MW01688204

The Art Of
KamaSutra

THE ART OF

KAMASUTRA

SHANKAR BARUA

All rights are reserved. No part of this publication may be transmitted or reproduced in any form or by any means without the prior permission of the publisher.

ISBN: 0-86288-557-4

Page 2: *If a girl loves a man, she should use all her charms to ensnare him. If she has many suitors, she should choose the one who loves her the most.*

Pages 6-7: *Harems are well guarded, and no man except the king may enter them. All the women live there, and they often resort to subterfuges such as smuggling in a young beardless man, disguised as a woman, to give them pleasure.*

Pages 8-9: *The first wife must never treat a new wife as a rival. She should use all her charm and instruct the newcomer in the arts of lovemaking, in such a way as to be overheard by her husband.*

CONTENTS

*

A man looking for a bride must choose a well-bred virgin of his own caste and community who is three years younger than him. Her living parents must prove that they have brought her up strictly.

CHAPTER 1

VATSYAYANA'S LOST CHAPTER REINVENTED

It is an ancient golden rule that the actions of good men and women are always guided by their own enlightened interpretations of what is right, and what is wrong. In this, allowance is always made for variation in the prevailing circumstance, mores, norms, traditions, and values, of the heritage and society the individual has sprung from, and that which he or she lives in.

The most sacred ancient texts of India propose the simple exaltation, based on knowledge, as the purest exercise of logic in life and worship. It is an irresistible argument to the initiated, for the only goals thus, are humility, harmony, and happiness; the outward manifestations of what we refer to as good *dharma*, *artha* and *kama*. All seem irreproachably virtuous and dependent on no sacrifice, thus standing firmly as the measuring rods of all men, and all women.

However, most interrelationships among sentient individuals emerge from encounters between essentially independent, separate and inescapably varying perspectives and compulsions. Good relationships thus formed and maintained, are thereby always dependent upon mutual negotiation, adjustment, acceptance, trust, sacrifice, and happiness, in a sort of reciprocal exaltation between individual beings.

Beyond this, it has always been seen fit, among all communities, to define those relationships attending the circumstances of one's birth, in non-negotiable terms. Thus, rights, responsibilities, and a basic hierarchy in the structure of individual family units, are expected to conform to some shared code of basic honourable conduct in every society.

In the essentially unequal sexual encounter between a man and a woman, it is only a foundation of faith, trust and ethical sexual union that allows them to transcend the elementary rutting of beasts.

Likewise, broad social codes in the larger structure of individual communities are also dictated, for in the harmony of these lies the foundation of societies and civilisations.

The only two classes of adult interrelationship never socially dictated to — their being left almost entirely instead to negotiation between the individuals concerned — are that between friends, and that between lovers. In these, it would seem that nothing much need be said, for all the drives of *dharma*, *artha*, and *kama*, are in any case to attend the actions and relationships of all good men and good women.

On the other hand, it can be observed that although each is always unique, every good friendship rests upon some perceived equality in the joint pursuit of pleasures and common purpose, without profound mutual agreement or commitment. True friendship always remains open to multiplicity, and is free from any great adjustment or interdependence. It contains very limited potential for causing harm and damage to the psyche of either party and is therefore a free, light, and pleasant pursuit for everybody. Of course, that proximity between individuals which attends all friendship allows for harsh damage from treachery, but this is a matter of individual cases where there is betrayal of friendship, rather than a matter of friendship itself, and is restricted to the actions of dishonourable individuals, lunatics, and plain fools.

Now, although there is much common foundation in the relationships between friends and those between lovers, the seminal joint pursuit of pleasures and common purpose among lovers is the altogether unique adventure of sexual intercourse with each other. In the simplest terms, this is a mating of physical and psychological differentials between individuals, as epitomised in the invasive character of the eventual penetration of woman by man; a symbolically perfect union of opposites. There is stoutness expected of men, and there is softness expected of women; an implicit aggression matched to an explicit acceptance.

While the primary drives of both lovers must obviously converge to initiate good sex, even the most basic conceptual implications immediately diverge. In the natural state, for example, whereas the man is physically free to reject all responsibility for any consequences of the act and move on, the woman may very well have already entered into the long chain of obligations and reduced freedoms implicit in a pregnancy (for no safe birth-control technique is one hundred per cent proof, or natural). In fact, the animal drive and genetic urge towards procreation — or just survival of the species — which lies at the deepest root of all sexual union, rests upon an inescapable physical interdependence across this huge differential for its fulfilment in the natural course. Sociobiologists call it simply the cost of reproduction. To cap all this, there are historically widespread social codes that — some would say consequently — reward the sexually adventurous man with honour, and the sexually adventurous woman with dishonour.

In the essentially unequal sexual encounter between lovers, it is only a foundation of faith, trust, and ethical sexual acumen that will allow them to transcend the elementary rutting of beasts, into a domain of mutual respect, love, and consequently profound pleasure. The truly joyous sexual act then becomes sacramental to a relationship, 'the outward sign of an inner grace' worth aspiring for. Those deeply fulfilling relationships which achieve this are impossible to sustain between a multiplicity of partners, and the interdependency of spirit thus manifested introduces a potential for very grevious psychological injury from even the ignorance or plain idiocy of either or both the lovers. The stakes are therefore too high to allow much concession for even 'innocence beyond a very early point of time in the evolution and progression of a relationship between lovers'.

As girls are not familiar with sexual union, they should be treated with gentleness, and the man should display considerable restraint at the beginning of their relationship.

*

The most neglected wife should not lose heart. She should be cheerful at all times, caring for the children of the other wives as if they were her own. She must make a very special effort to be passionate in bed even if her husband leaves her cold, and gradually she will find him turning his attention to her.

Societies all over the world responded to these potential dangers in the game of love by establishing institutions of marriage in the distant mists of prehistory. In time, marriages came to be celebrated as one of the first logical goals in a respectable and safe relationship between lovers. It was only within marriage after all, that the individual long-term roles and responsibilities of lovers could finally be delineated according to the values of a society, thus reducing the risk-potentials of their interdependence to a very great degree. Such social institutions have therefore survived almost intact to our day.

Beyond outlining rules in the institution of marriage, however, the ancient sages of India realised that individual sexual relationships between lovers were too unique and too private to ever be dictated to, although many societies have attempted to do so throughout history. They also understood that the absence of sexual happiness in an otherwise perfect marriage could often reduce the institution to serving a terrible bondage, to unhappiness and even suffering. Accumulated wisdom could not generally adjudicate in these matters, but it could (as every good parent should attempt for his, or her, children) share the simple knowledge that may avert such tragedy, before the event.

Young girls should receive sex instruction from an older married female relative, friend or old female servant.

Along these lines, the first Kamashastra is ascribed to Nandi, companion of Shiva — the Lord of Destruction — who is always joined with his consort Parvati, as the supreme symbol of perfection in the unity of contrasts. Nandi's original 1,000 chapters were condensed into 500 by Shvetaketu. Then Babhravya rendered this in 150 chapters, under seven heads. Of these, the general topics were expounded upon by Charanya; embraces, pressing, scratching, biting, etc., were collated by Suvarnanabha; Ghotakamukha addressed sexual union; Gonardiya spoke on one's wife, Gonikaputra on the wives of others, and Dattaka addressed the public women of Pataliputra, at their request, about courtesans. The knowledge of sex aids, tonics, elixirs, medicine and magic was compiled by Kuchumara, and the seven parts were then gathered into thirty-six chapters (of which the first is lost) by Vatsyayana.

Vatsyayana's *Kamasutra* has been in Indian circulation as an academic treatise for some eighteen hundred years now, but in the last one hundred, archaic translations have been reproduced and sold all over the world to merely titillate tastes that approach sex as something surreptitious and lewd; to be hidden beneath covers, or peeped at. Today, *The Art of Kamasutra* takes up the old wisdom on the pleasures of enlightened indulgence, to remould them by the norms, needs, and language of a new age. This chapter has been concocted to fill in for the lost one of the original, but the rest is rewritten with varied modification, straightforward appropriation, some addition, and selective omission, from the translation of F. F. Arbuthnot and Sir Richard Burton. It is therefore fitting that we now begin from a very slightly rewritten version of their original rendition of Vatsyayana's conclusion:

'Thus have I written in a few words these aphorisms on love, after reading ancient texts and following in the ways of enjoyment taught in them.'

Girls should learn about sexual matters from books and other sources, before and after they are married.

विरहविदितमंतःप्रेमविज्ञायकांतः पुनरपिवसुतस्मादेत्य
मेदास्यतीति॥मरिचनियमहत्वेणोन्यस्यबाष्पोदबिंदून्विसृष्टऽति
पुरयोषिद्वारदेशोपविष्टा॥ ॥:॥
सामान्यवनिता
प्रोषितभर्तृका

'One acquainted with the true principles of this science pays regard to *dharma*, *artha*, *kama*, past experience, and the teachings of others, never acting simply by the dictates of his own desire. As for errors in the science of love contained in this work, I have acted on my own authority as author, to immediately censure and prohibit them.

'An action is never indulged in simply because it is authorised by the science, for it must be remembered that the intent always is that rules contained should be acted upon only when appropriate. This *Kamasutra* has been composed after reading, considering, and thinking over the meaning of the rules given in the works of Babhravya and other ancient authors, according to the precepts of holy writ, for the benefit of the world, by Vatsyayana, while leading the life of a religious student wholly engaged in contemplation of the deity.

'The work is not intended merely to be used as an instrument for satisfying our desires. Rather, a person acquainted with the true principles of this science, and who preserves his *dharma*, *artha*, and *kama*, has regard for the practices of the people, and is sure to have a mastery of his senses.

'In short, an intelligent and prudent person, attending to *dharma* and *artha*, and attending also to *kama*, without becoming a slave to his passions, obtains success in everything he may undertake.'

Knowledge regarding a range of subjects makes a woman attractive to a man, and makes her personality well rounded. An articulate and gallant man wins the hearts of women.

Facing page: *The chambers of a house should be divided to suit different purposes. There should be adequate privacy for women, ample open space, and a garden.*

On *dharma*, *artha*, and *kama*

It has long been thought good that one should rigorously pursue the life of a student through the years of one's childhood, until done with one's education. One should take care to learn from philosophical, political, historical and religious scriptures, and from those learned in the scriptures, to justly conjure one's own vision of *dharma*. One should pay heed to teachers and all successful people, to understand the ways of the world, and to choose one's own role in the pursuit of *artha*. One should learn from the books of pleasure, and the practices of citizens, to always associate the senses with the mind and soul, so that the consciousness of pleasure arising from the peculiar contact between an organ of sense and its object, shall always let you know *kama*.

Accordingly, *dharma* is the perceived writ which defines and dictates religious duties alongside social rights, responsibilities and goals of virtue and religious merit: *artha* addresses correctness of material status and being its maintenance, use and enhancement: *kama* is of perfection in the exploitation and use of sense and the senses in pursuit of earned pleasures, beyond the limited potential of just abject surrender to the basic animal drives of instinct, passion and sensual gratification.

After having been educated, the pursuit of *artha* and *kama* is correct and proper through youth and middle age, and *dharma* should be paramount in old age. But it is allowed that you should also always practise what circumstances demand and dictate. In this, it must, however, be remembered that when opportunities for all coincide, it is better to pursue *dharma* over *artha* and *kama*, and when just the two are before you, the pursuit of *artha* is nobler than the pursuit of *kama*. Exceptions to this are generally allowed in only two cases; kings and leaders of government shall commit themselves first to *artha*, for on this is based the livelihood of men, and prostitutes and public women shall serve *kama* first, for to do so is their profession.

Dharma must be learned by all because at the root of all religion there is a universal holy writ on what is good, and what is bad, which does not admit of any doubt. Just as the universe is ordered, so too is our existence dependent upon the general observance of certain principles in the behaviour of men and women. Just as a seed is sown to produce a plant, and as every action produces a reaction, so too does every one of our deeds yield some crop in the future.

Artha must be learned by all because all acquisition presupposes exertion. Ends

Some time should be spent every day with other women from whom one can learn something; women who are interesting companions, and with whom one can have a good conversation.

are gained in life by applying proper means. The man who does nothing, gains nothing, and this is always true of even just happiness.

Kama must be learned by all because pleasures are as necessary as food for one's existence and well being, and are consequently required equally. Pleasures are in fact the first fruits of good *dharma* and *artha*, but they must be pursued with a moderation and caution born of knowledge. In sexual matters, the solely instinctual approach of brute creation embodies a lack of restraint, a subservience to seasons, and limited thinking ability.

Practising a balance of good *dharma*, *artha* and *kama*, is obviously the simple road to earned success and a lasting happiness in life. The good never act to the detriment of their own welfare, or the welfare of others. Any act that serves good *dharma*, *artha* and *kama*, or any two, or even one of them, is a good act to perform. But any act which serves any one at the expense of the other two, should never be performed. Finally, it must always be remembered that the practice and pursuit of *kama* alone, destroys.

On education and preparation for adulthood

All men and women should study the arts and subordinate sciences of *kama*, in addition to those of *artha* and *aharma*, as a part of their education in the normal course. Even young girls should study sexual matters before marriage, and then continue to do so after marriage with the knowledge of their husbands, for in any case, all men and women already know and instinctively act upon the basics. In this, as in much else, a great many things are done by people from instinct, practice and custom alone, without any

acquaintance with reasons or the laws on which they are based.

Just as riders of horses and elephants know how to train their animals without being professional trainers themselves, so too are very many of even the most well-bred of ladies adroit in sexual matters, without being prostitutes. On the other hand, whereas vast and varied experience is the general basis of a trainer's or a prostitute's talents, this cannot be recommended in sexual matters for everybody. In fact, it is stressed that although sexual matters should be studied, this must be done alongside the study of full sixty-four other subjects, from martial arts and reasoning or inferring, to commerce, singing, observing social protocol, debating, and other social or simple practical graces. Also, in sexual matters, there is wisdom in the ancient recommendation that unmarried women should study these in private under the tutelage of an aunt, a trustworthy female friend, a sister, or an old female servant, etc., all of whom it is said should be married.

Even a public woman with such a full education, and given a good disposition along with other winning qualities, wins respect and universal regard in society. Among other women, such a background allows them to render husbands and lovers totally favourable to themselves, and equips them to look after themselves even when alone in the most distressful of situations.

Knowledge on a range of topics, in a well-rounded personality, has always lent attractiveness to women. As for men — when loquacious and gallant, and well versed in a variety of topics and the arts and sciences of *kama* — well, they will easily win over the hearts of women.

Visit and become acquainted with people worth knowing, converse with them, please friends by spending time with them, and help those who need your assistance.

On the life of a citizen

It was earlier always thought best for a woman to remain with her parents until she married. These days, this has changed somewhat, and a woman may very well take the course that was always recommended for a man.

After completing your education, you should muster your wealth and resources to become a householder, and live the life of an independent citizen. You should ideally take a house near water in a respectable community, or at least in the vicinity of good men and women. Divide the chambers of your house to suit different uses, leaving adequate areas for the privacy of ladies, and making sure of open space for fresh air and some form of garden. You should have a living room, well appointed with comforts, diversions, and simple sensory stimuli such as music, flowers, fetishes, drawing-pads and pencils, comfortable couches and chairs, musical instruments, paintings, fruit and other things to nibble, some aromatic fragrance or air freshener, etc. If you have enough open space, maintain swings, hammocks, hanging chairs, a stone bench in some romantic nook, and a shed or at least some small covered area, for the pursuit of crafts and hobbies.

Your days should be structured so that whether it be in the pursuit of pleasures, responsibility, or exigency, your time is always optimised and well utilised. Attend to your entire toilette first thing in the morning: flush your bowels, bathe with particular attention to your armpits and crotch, shave, perfume yourself, apply skin lotions, pungents, the make-up of your preference, etc., and round it off with something to lend fragrance to your breath. In your daily bath, you should also oil your skin every second day, use soap and shampoo every third day, trim hair every fourth day, and depilate body hair (if you do so) at least once every ten days.

Spend some time every day attending to the aesthetics of your home, and some time with persons of your own sex whom you can learn something from, be entertained by, and carry on a good conversation with. Commit yourself to a daily work schedule, and always make a point of dressing up well for dealings with friends, colleagues, and for business matters. In the evening, take in some entertainment such as music, and then join a friend of your own sex in entertaining and courting your respective lovers with conversation.

Aside from such everyday affairs, you should play a full role in society by participating in the production of neighbourhood festivals, public entertainments, religious rites, etc., and make a point of tipping good performers on the next day. You should attend and

The best friends are those who are always loyal and true; whom time and other people cannot change; those who are sympathetic, can keep secrets, and are never jealous.

organise gatherings of likeminded folk, where good conversation flows, and where respectable men and women interact on a social plane. Do occasionally go on a spree with friends, and drink heartily, but do not invite wives and lovers to such occasions. Commit a day here and there to outdoor activities to celebrate seasons, pluck fruit, spend moonlit nights outdoors, picnic, play, and camp in forests. Call on, and get to know people worth knowing, converse in company, gratify friends by your society, oblige others with aid and various kinds of assistance, and help others to assist one another.

A citizen who speaks
Neither highbrow nor low
On the various topics in society
Gains respect.
The wise will shun the company
Of those generally disliked
Who seem governed by no rules
And are intent on the destruction of others.
The learned are highly respected
When embracing the company of those
Whose pursuit of pleasure never strays
Beyond the acceptable norms of society.

On sexual partners, and on friends and messengers

When sexual pleasures are pursued in a respectable marriage between social equals, it becomes a means to acquire lawful

For men, the pursuit of a purely sexual relationship is permitted with only four general categories of women — young, unattached and promiscuous women, women who have been married twice without having been widowed, public women, and those who are resorted to for purposes other than propagation of progeny or pleasure.

progeny and good repute in accordance with the customs of the world. Purely sexual liaisons with promiscuous men or women from families such as your own will generally be looked upon disapprovingly.

For men, the pursuit of solely sexual pleasure is legitimate (that is, not sinful) with only four broad categories of women: 1. young unattached women who are not promiscuous; 2. women twice-married without having been widowed; 3. public women, and 4. women resorted to for some special purpose other than pleasure or progeny.

There are, on the other hand, quite a few categories of women who are specifically prohibited to men for sexual encounters (women will find that this may also serve as a good benchmark for them). The categories are: 1. those with a sexually communicable disease; 2. lunatics; 3. social outcasts; 4. those who reveal secrets; 5. those who publicly express sexual desires; 6. those who are exceedingly pale, or dark (according to the norms of the community); 7. bad-smelling individuals; 8. near relatives; 9. friends of the opposite sex; 10. ascetics, and 11. the spouses of relatives, friends, socially respected persons, and kings or leaders of government.

Of all in the last category, Babhravya held that the ethical foundation was redundant when applied to a woman who has had sexual intercourse with at least five men. Gonikaputra accepted Babhravya's argument as a general precept, but insisted that these exceptions should nevertheless stand on purely ethical grounds.

Have messengers and friends one can always depend on, who are intelligent, confident, unafraid and ever courteous.

Of friends it is said that the following are the best: 1. childhood friends; 2. those bound by obligation; 3. those of the same disposition; 4. fellow students; 5. those who know your secrets and faults very well, just as you know theirs; 6. your nurse's child; 7. one brought up with you, and 8. those whose families share an old friendship with yours. Beyond this, the best of friends will always be true to you, unchanged by time, favouring your designs, firm, uncovetuous, never gained over by others, and keeping secrets well.

For messengers and representatives you may depend upon, seek those who be skilful, bold, never confused or shy, and always well-mannered. They should be able to anticipate a person's intentions by observation, read meaning into word and action,

understand appropriateness of time and place, and have business ingenuity and keen comprehension, with quick and ready resources and remedies.

A man who is ingenious and wise
Always accompanied by a friend
And knowing well the intentions of others
As well as the proper time and place for everything
Can gain over
Even a woman
Who is very hard to be obtained.

A friend should be intuitive, observant, have a finely-tuned sense of timing and appropriateness of place. She must be ingenuous, with keen comprehension and a ready wit.

*

According to Vatsyayana, moderation and restraint should be exercised at the first coupling. Thereafter, it is unnecessary.

Pages 28-29: *Even a courtesan with a fully-developed personality and a sound education, who has an amiable disposition and winning ways, gains the respect and regard of people.*

CHAPTER 2

ON SEXUAL UNION

It is no secret that men differ from each other in the sizes of their phalli. We may therefore broadly categorise the various sizes of phalli among men as small, medium and large. Similarly we may categorise the capaciousness of the vaginas of women as small, medium and large too. Now given that the two are intended to be fit each other, we can presume that a small phallus is ideally matched to a small vagina, a medium-sized phallus to a medium-sized vagina, and a large phallus to a large vagina. Let these combinations of sexual organs in coitus then be known as the three equal unions between men and women.

In line with this simple formula, six other combinations of sexual organs are also possible by matching the one of a particular size to the other of a size that does not correspond to it. Let these combinations of sexual organs be known as the six unequal unions between men and women, and we shall have a total of nine possible combinations.

Of these nine combinations, the best are the three equal unions. The next best are the three combinations of larger phalli to smaller vagina, in which good sexual intercourse is still generally possible without injury to the woman. These three combinations are therefore referred to as high unions. Of the remaining three combinations — of larger vaginas to smaller phalli — the extremely contrasted cases can sometimes have the most demanding coitus to deal with, as it may be hard to satisfy the woman by any means, and so these are known as low unions.

Again, it is no secret that people differ from each other in the levels of their passion and carnal desire. Individual men and women may have small passion, with little proclivity at any time towards embraces, kisses and the like, and no great desire even during intercourse, or, they may have middling passion by differing from this, or they may have intense passion and be always full of desire. Thus we find that there also are nine possible combinations by levels of passion in the coitus of lovers.

The same is true for the time it takes individuals to satisfactorily conclude sexual intercourse with orgasm, but there was much ancient debate on this. Auddalika held that men ejaculate and cease of themselves, while women do not ejaculate, cannot describe their pleasure, and do not seem to cease of themselves. This proposition was objected to on the plea that women in general preferred long intercourse. This in turn was objected to with the claim that, unlike the more spontaneous arousal and abrupt satiation of men in coitus, the desire and passion of women takes some time to be fully aroused, and so they naturally often seem to wish continuation. The following verse was then introduced into the debate:

> By union with men
> The lust, desire, or passion
> Of women is satisfied
> And the pleasure derived
> From the consciousness of it
> Is called their satisfaction.

Babhravya's followers then arose to equate the vaginal lubricating juices of women with the man's ejaculate, proposing that it was equally contributory to conception (remember that this was almost two thousand years ago). Thus they held that whereas the man climaxes with a sudden ejaculation in the natural process of procreation, the woman equally naturally anticipates him by climaxing continually throughout intercourse. This again was objected to on the ground that women begin coitus with a middling passion and cannot immediately bear vigorous thrusts, then their

Above and below: *Vatsyayana has reiterated that differences in the pleasure felt in sexual intercourse by man and woman is a convergence of the roles they play. He insisted, though, that the pleasure remains the same.*
Facing page: *A man begins the sexual act with passion and climaxes quickly. A woman, however, is slow to passion, and takes long to climax.*

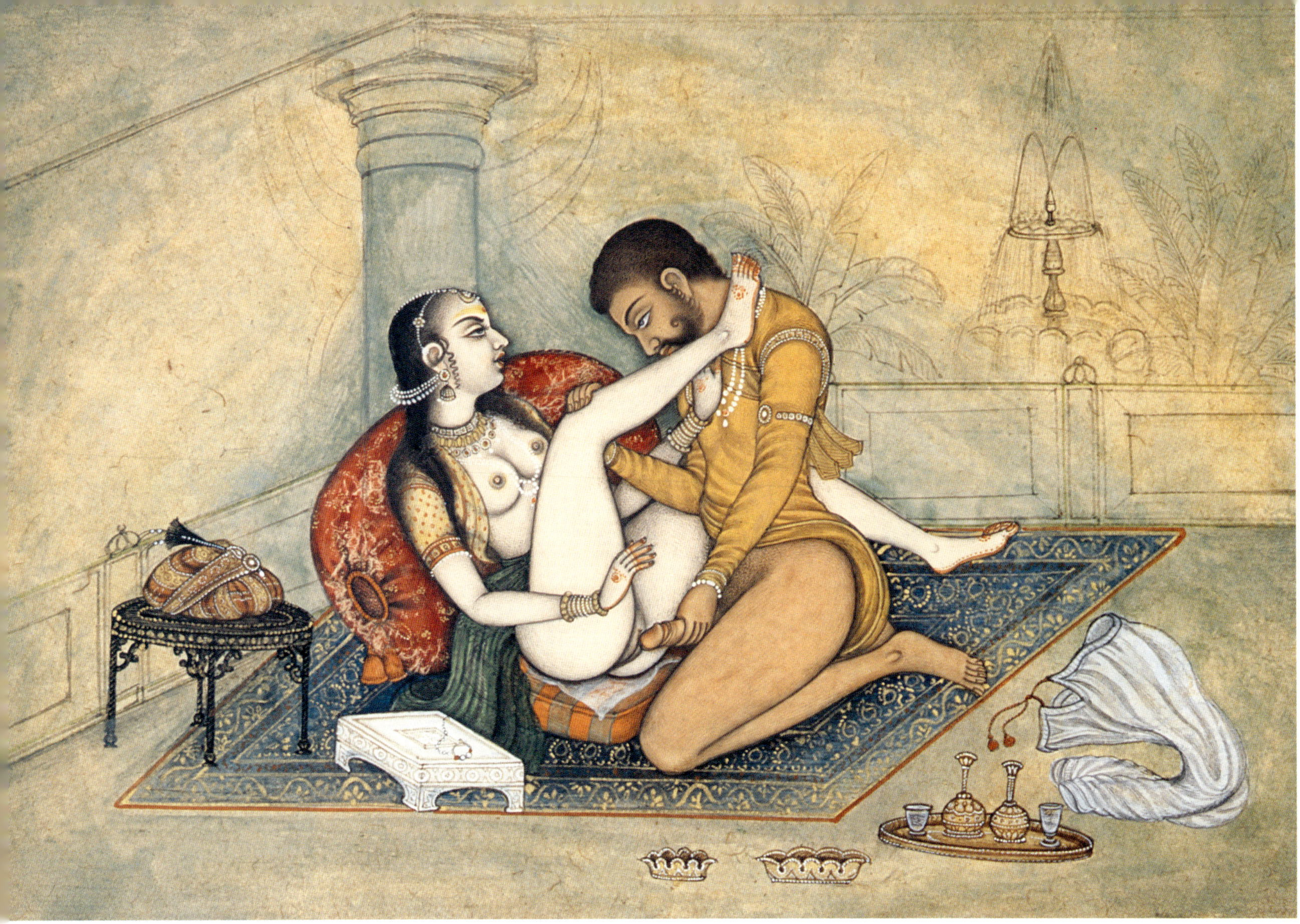

Sexual intercourse in which each partner fully enjoys each other and the occasion, and is fully satisfied with each other, in the best possible union.

passion increases by degrees till they are unconcerned about their bodies, and finally they do wish to stop. That point was received by the declaration that such a sequence is but a matter of the laws of momentum observable in very many things, and the following verse was submitted:

The man's juices flow
Only at the end of coitus
While the juices of women
Flow continually.
When the juices of both
Have fallen away
Then they wish
For discontinuation.

Vatsyayana himself laid down that differences in the consciousness of pleasure in sexual intercourse could logically be inferred from the different physical roles played by the man and the woman, but he insisted that whether it was less or more, the pleasure itself remains the same, for it is derived from the same act. Holding that the critical factor was something else, he offered the following verse:

Men and women
Being of the same human nature
Feel the same kinds of pleasure.
Therefore
A man should marry
Such a woman
As will always love him.

There are various kinds of sexual love — the kind that follows the course of habit, the one which arises from novelty of concept, partner or technique; and finally, there is sexual love, where the man and woman intensely love and enjoy each other.

Innumerable combinations are possible in every sexual relationship. Therefore, partners should keep their minds open to a range of possibilities suitable to the occasion.

At any rate, we can readily accept that there are nine different possible combinations between sexual partners in terms of whether it takes each a little, not so little, or a long time to climax in coitus.

With nine separate possible combinations each — of sexual partners — by just dimension, force of passion, and time, innumerable combinations become possible in considering all three within every different relationship. Therefore, in each kind of sexual encounter, both partners should open their minds to all such means as are suitable to the occasion.

Beyond this, remember the added complication that in a series of couplings between the same partners over a relatively short span of time — such as a single night, or day — the man will begin with intense passion, and climax quickly, but will go on with a reducing passion at each successive coupling and a corresponding increase in the time it takes him to climax. A woman on the other hand will begin with weak passion and take a long time to climax, but will go on to each successive coupling with increasing passion and quicker climaxes, until she is fully satiated.

During coitus, lovers should twist their arms and legs around each other, and both should embrace each other as if they were trying to merge into each other.

Finally, there are various different kinds of sexual love. There is the sexual love that follows the course of habit, as is found in many old lovers; there is the sexual love arising from novelty of concept, partner, or technique; there is the sexual love that emerges from believing that you share a true mutual love, and, there is the sexual love in which you truly and deeply enjoy your partner and the occasion, and desire nothing better from either.

The last, needless to say, is the best.

On the embrace

Babhravya proposed that the various components of sexual intercourse can be discussed within the following eight subjects: sexual embraces; kissing; scratching; biting; lying down; making sounds; playing the part of a man, and, oral sex. He further proposed that each of these subjects dealt with eight specific elements, thereby totalling up to the 64 arts of *kama*. Vatsyayana held that this simple formula was inadequate,

and affirmed that one must also consider striking, crying, the man's role in coitus, the various modes of coitus, and other subjects.

On sexual embraces, as dealt with by Vatsyayana, the first two occur with two people who do not as yet speak freely to each other. In a touching embrace, the man brushes against the woman's body, on any adequate pretext. In a piercing embrace, the woman seemingly accidentally crushes her breasts against the man, and he in turn quickly puts his hands to them for an instant, as if instinctively to steady her.

For two people who share and know each other's intent, there are two more embraces. In a rubbing embrace the two potential lovers consciously rub their bodies against each other while walking together. In a pressing embrace, one of the lovers purposely presses the other's body against a wall, pillar, or any other solid and stable thing, with his or her own body, in an everyday situation such as looking down at a river over the railing of a bridge.

It was considered de rigueur that a nobleman wanting to impress a lady would take her on a hunt to impress her with his hunting prowess before pressing his suit.

Upon the meeting of lovers, the woman may twine like a creeper around the man while standing, cling to him, look up to him lovingly, and draw his face down to hers for a kiss, making little kissing sounds in the air all the while. In the 'climbing of a tree', she will also sling a leg around the man's thigh, and seem to climb him.

Finally, during coitus, lovers may embrace closely, and twine legs and arms about each other, like a 'mixture of sesame seed and rice', and both may urgently squeeze each other to themselves as if seeking to merge into one, like a 'mix of milk and rice'.

Suvarnanabha adds that one may squeeze a lover's leg between one's own; the man may pull the woman hips and loins towards his own when mounting her; he may press his chest down between her breasts, and either may touch the other's eyes, mouth, and forehead, etc., with his or her own.

Embraces are such
That men who ask
Hear
Or talk of it
Are thereby aroused.

Even embraces mentioned nowhere
Should be practiced in coitus
If they increase love
And passion.

Rules of the Shastra
Are good
With middling passion,
But when the wheel of love
Is fully set rolling
Then there is no Shastra
And no order.

On kissing

Some of the ancient commentators on *kama* held that embracing, kissing, pressing and scratching may be done in any order before sexual union, while striking and making sounds should be reserved for coitus. Vatsyayana, however, dismissed this, holding that love does not care for time or order.

He nevertheless points out that in a first coupling, everything should be done in moderation, separately and alternately. But in subsequent coitus, reserve and

Just as riders of horses and elephants are adept at training their animals, so are many well-bred ladies adroit in sexual matters, without being prostitutes.

moderation are unnecessary, and all things agreeable to both lovers may even be done simultaneously to kindle love, desire and passion. Kisses are ideally placed on each other's forehead, eyes, cheeks, throat, bosom, breasts, lips, and the inside of the mouth. Others parts recommended, suitable for some, but not fit for all, are the joints of the thighs, the arms and the navel.

When kissing a lover, a young girl may just gently touch his lips with her own in a nominal kiss, or when a little less bashful, she may move her lower lip against his, quietly feeling and stroking it in a throbbing kiss, and she may close her eyes, hold her lover's hands, and run her tongue against and between his lips in a 'touching kiss'.

Of other kisses, it is said that you may bring your lips directly into contact with your lover's in a 'straight kiss'; you may bend and reach towards each other for a 'bent kiss'; you may draw and turn your lover's face towards your own, with a hand, for a 'turned kiss'; you may squeeze your lover's lower lip between your own in a 'pressed kiss', and even pull it forward with your fingers to do so more vigorously in a 'greatly pressed kiss'; the man may kiss his lover's upper lip while she kisses his lower lip in a 'kiss of the upper lip', and you may take your lover's entire lips into your own in a 'clasping kiss' (but women may not like it very much with a mustachioed man), and then rove about in your lover's mouth and play with his or her tongue with your own.

The various modes of sexual enjoyment are not appropriate for everyone, all the time. They should be indulged in only if they are acceptable to both partners.

Pages 40-41: *There is strength expected of men, and softness of women; an implicit agression matched to an explicit acceptance.*

Only intensely passionate lovers can make games of kissing itself, but all lovers should be aware that kisses become appropriate for different parts of the body by the tenderness or urgency, and the pressure, suction or softness applied.

Apart from physical variety in kissing, there are some kinds of kisses that are defined more by circumstance. A woman looking at a sleeping lover may give him the 'kiss that kindles desire', to serve her own intent and desire; a woman may give a cranky or otherwise occupied lover a 'kiss that turns (the mind) away'; a man coming home late may give his sleeping lover a 'kiss that awakens' (a woman may sometimes feign sleep for this, to know her lover's intent, and even have him court her afresh); one may demonstratively kiss the lover's picture or reflection with a 'kiss showing intention', and, one may give a 'transferred kiss' to a child in one's lap, or a doll, or pet, etc. Finally, when the man contrives to kiss the woman's hand, or any other body part he can clandestinely get at, in a public gathering, at a public place , or when the woman puts her head in the man's lap as if sleepy, and kisses his thigh or big toe to inflame his passion, in a private setting, it is a 'demonstrative kiss'.

Whatever be done
By one lover to another
The same should be returned
By that other;
If the woman kisses the man
He should kiss her
In return;
If she strikes him
He should strike her
In return.

On pressing, marking, and scratching

Vatsyayana observed that just as variety is necessary in a relationship between lovers, so too is love to be produced by means of variety. After all, if variety is sought in all the arts and amusements, surely it must also be sought in the arts and games of love. But he repeatedly cautioned that all things should only be done between lovers who both find it agreeable. In this vein, pressing, marking and scratching generally occur only between intensely passionate lovers, or in sexual encounters of intense love prompted by reunion, reconciliation, imminent separation (as when one of the lovers is to depart on a long journey), intoxication of the woman, or in the first coitus between lovers. In any case, it is necessary that you avoid these arts if you have unattractive or dirty hands and nails.

There are innumerable ways to mark a lover with a 'token of remembrance', but these should obviously be very consciously limited to only the most private parts on the body of a lover married to someone else. Other than that, such marks seen in a woman's cleavage, or on her neck by a stranger, are said to fill him with respect and affection for her, and the same is said of the reaction of women, to men so marked.

On the other hand, one need not always leave a mark when using one's nails on a

When there is no magic, no poetry and no playfulness between a man and a woman in their lovemaking, it is a lifeless, dead thing.

lover. In 'sounding' for example, you may just drag a nail gently across the chin, breasts, lower lip, or the middle body of a young girl — making her hair stand erect — to trouble, tease, or playfully frighten her. In the same way, the following may be done firmly or softly, or not done at all, according to the disposition of both lovers: You may dig a single nail into the neck and breasts of your lover to leave a 'half moon'; pinch two half moons to make a circle on the navel, joints of the thigh, or in the dimples of the buttocks; you may scratch a line anywhere; curve a line into a tiger's tail on the breast; squeeze a peacock's foot into the lover's breast with all five nails of a hand to impress her (but this needs skill); squeeze all five nails close to each other, around a nipple, in 'the jump of a hare', and, pinch together a bit of skin on the hip or breast for the mark of a 'leaf of the blue lotus'.

A woman's love
Arises afresh and anew
Upon seeing
Her lover's
Old and new marks
On her body.

When the passage of love
Is unmarked by marks
Then love lessens
As though union has not occurred
Awhile.

On biting, and means to be employed with regard to women of different countries

All places that can be kissed can be bitten too, except the upper lip, inner mouth and the eyes. But biting is another one of the arts of love which is appropriate for only some kinds of lovers. Again, this is an art which may be practised only by those with attractive, unbroken and clean teeth.

The various kinds of love bites are as follows:

The 'hidden bite' leaves only a redness of the lower lip; the 'swollen bite' leaves the skin depressed around the lower lip or on the left cheek (Vatsyayana insists that kissing,

Facing page and above: *In sexual intercourse, the positions assumed by the lovers are very important. They add zest to lovemaking and make it vibrant and exciting.*

scratching and biting are ornaments of only the left cheek); in the 'point' one pinches a bit of the lover's lower lip between two teeth, and you may do the same with a few teeth on the skin of the throat, underarm, joints of the thigh, forehead and the thighs, for a 'line of points'; the 'coral and jewel' is made by biting the lover's cheek between teeth (for jewels) and lips (for the coral), and, you may take a bite of skin between your teeth on the throat, underarm, or joints of your lover's thighs for a 'line of jewels'. Of people of intense passion it is said that one may press impressions of the face of the teeth onto the lover's breast in a 'broken cloud', and one may leave many broad rows of marks near each other, with red intervals, from the 'biting of a boar' on breasts and shoulders.

On the other hand, you may instead (or also) kiss, bite and scratch your lover's ornaments.

Coitus which takes place between two people who are sexually attracted to each other, and which is done according to their mutual liking, is called 'spontaneous congress'.

Now, all women are differently disposed towards sex, and the arts of sex, by their individual preferences, and the customs of the lands they belong to and live in. Accordingly, for example, they may be of noble character; be unaccustomed to peculiar and disgraceful practices; dislike kissing, scratching, squeezing and biting; be easily gained over by striking; enjoy foul pleasures; have bad manners; be fond of all the arts, like verbalising during coitus, variety of love, and enjoy embracing, kissing and striking; enjoy oral sex; be full of passion and slow kisses; lubricate vaginally in large measure and enjoy mood-modifiers before coitus; have tender bodies; be fond of all enjoyments; love voluptuous pleasures, and speak sweetly, etc.

Suvarnanabha advises that whatever is agreeable to the nature of a particular person is of more consequence in love than what is agreeable to a nation. But he cautions that in the sequence of the arts, kissing and embracing, etc., must come first to increase passion, and only then should one go on to activities for amusement and variety.

When your man bites you forcibly
Bite him back with double force
Answering a 'point' with a 'line of points'
Or a 'line of points' with a 'broken cloud'.

If ye be excessively chaffed
Start a love quarrel and hold his hair

To pull his face to you
Kiss his lower lip
Shut your eyes
And bite him
In various places.

Even by day in a public place
If your lover shows you marks made by you
Smile and turn to chide him
And with angry looks
Show the marks he has made on you.
Thus
If man and woman
Act according to each other's liking
Their love for each other

Whereas in equal unions the organs match, unequal unions may sometimes require special accommodation during sexual intercourse.

Will not lessen
Even in one hundred years.

On different positions and different kinds of coitus

We have already noted that there are different sizes of vaginas and phalli among women and men, and that there can therefore be equal and unequal unions of the two. Whereas in equal unions the organs match well, thus allowing a full variety of mutually satisfactory approaches to coitus, unequal unions may sometimes require special accommodation because of the different sizes being dealt with.

Babhravya recommends that in high union — when the man's phallus is large, and the woman's vagina small — the woman may assume either of three positions when lying on her back for coitus. In the 'widely opened position', her hips and crotch should be raised higher than the level of her head on a pillow or cushion, with her legs comfortably spread, and some lubricating substance should be applied by the man before coitus. In the 'yawning position', the woman may instead draw in her feet halfway towards her buttocks, raising her bent knees for the man to approach between her thighs. In the 'position of Indra's wife', Indrani, the woman draws her knees apart at her chest, and angles her lower legs and feet outwards in the air to the maximum extent possible, along the backs and outer sides of her thighs. This last position is said to require suppleness and practice, and is suitable for the highest union, where a very large phallus is matched to a very small vagina. In all cases, it is clear that the woman attempts to open up her vagina for the large phallus by adjusting her position.

Facing page: *There are numerous possible combinations of postures that lovers can assume during their lovemaking, depending on their inclination and desire.*

For low union — when the man's phallus is small, and the woman's vagina large — Babhravya recommends that there has to be special effort made for a suitably tight fit (he also says that some medicine may be helpful for satisfaction of the woman's desire). The woman may assume the 'clasping position' on her back, or on her side (Vatsyayana recommends for some reason that women should lie on their right side, and men on their left), by holding her legs together directly under or alongside the man's. She may then grip the man's phallus in her vagina by squeezing her thighs together, or twine a leg over him to clasp his phallus with her vagina in the 'mares position'. That last talent is arrived at by practice and effort alone, but is said to be common among women in some places.

Suvarnanabha adds — without discussing appropriateness by size — that a woman on her back may raise her legs straight into the air for the man to clasp them to his chest or shoulders with his hands, and approach from behind her thighs in the 'rising position', and she may even cross her thighs while doing so to assume the 'packed position'; raise

her legs onto the man's shoulders in the 'yawning position' (see above); bend her knees together and raise them in the air, so her lover may hold her contracted legs up against

his stomach and chest in the 'pressed position', or she may draw them down against her own chest in the 'crab position'; she may do this with just one leg, stretching out the other in the 'half pressed position'; or may alternate one leg on his shoulder with one outstretched in a 'splitting of the bamboo', or practise splits to eventually be able to bring her upper foot to his forehead so he can 'fix the nail', and she may cross her legs over each other, and draw them down to her stomach in a 'lotus-like position'.

The last position described by Suvarnanabha, called the 'turning position', is perhaps the most difficult in the entire arts of *kama*, and requires practice. It serves very well as a lesson that very many of the various arts of *kama* are not entirely appropriate for everybody, and should not even be attempted at all, if disliked. In this position, the woman has her legs bent and drawn over her head — her knees alongside her ears and her nether regions held high directly over her face — with almost her entire weight placed on the back of her neck and shoulders. Since her lover is to approach between her knees with his calves under her upper arms, holding her crotch up and against his own by her hips, this position is arrived at by first achieving union alongside each other, with faces towards feet, and then gradually turning around (thereby the name) into position without leaving each other. Needless to say, all kissing, embracing, caressing, and squeezing, etc., in this position is limited to each other's buttocks and backs, but some lovers will find it highly erotic to have such a close look at the actual conjunction of their sexual organs (on the other hand, be careful that the lady doesn't break her neck!). A more viable variation of this position could have the woman on her knees, holding her buttocks high, with her face laid down comfortably on the backs of her hands.

Pleasures are the first forms of dharma *and* artha*, but they must be pursued with moderation and caution born of knowledge.*

Suvarnanabha had recommended that lovers should practise and learn the different coital positions in water, but Vatsyayana objected that it was improper to do so as this was prohibited by religious law. Vatsyayana also listed eight kinds of coitus other than the traditional man on top, woman below:

1. The lovers may stand, supporting each other or leaning against a wall or pillar, in 'supported coitus'. In this position, the woman can make an adequate union easier by swinging either leg over the man's hip or thigh.

2. The man may hold up the woman entirely with his hands under her buttocks, lean back against a wall, and allow her to swing back and forth in the movements of coitus with her feet against the wall, in 'suspended coitus'.
3. The woman may stand on her hands and feet (or hands and knees), allowing the man to approach from behind in the 'coitus of a cow'. She can make herself more comfortable by resting her upper body on a table while standing, or on a bed when kneeling on the floor. She can even lie down partly on her side, with her upper leg drawn up higher than the lower, so the man may straddle the latter to still enter from behind, and yet have coitus almost face to face. In all the variations on this position, the man should do everything with his lover's buttocks that he would otherwise do with her breasts, and some lovers may even enjoy pretending to be different animals, with all the accompanying sounds.
4. A man may simultaneously enjoy two women, who love him equally, in 'united coitus'.

A man may enjoy a sexual encounter with several women. Similarly, a number of women can make love to a man — separately, alternately and severally. ***Page 52:*** *A woman on her back may raise her legs straight into the air and hold them wide apart in the 'yawning position'.*

5. He may enjoy many women together in the 'coitus of a herd of cows', but would do well to observe how different animals deal with such situations.
6. A number of men can approach a woman in a sexual encounter by enjoying her various parts separately and alternately.
7. In the same way, a number of women can approach a man in a sexual encounter by enjoying his various parts separately and alternately.
8. When a man inserts his phallus into the anus rather than the vagina of his lover, it is a 'lower coitus' not liked by most women. Some may, however, accept it as a birth-control method, some to preserve a deceitful virginity, and a few do actually enjoy it. If at all this is attempted for any reason, one should proceed with extreme caution and gentleness, ample extra lubrication, and a complete accord of intent between the lovers. The man should unfailingly and gently withdraw if requested to do so, and should wash thoroughly before inserting his phallus into his lover's vagina after this.

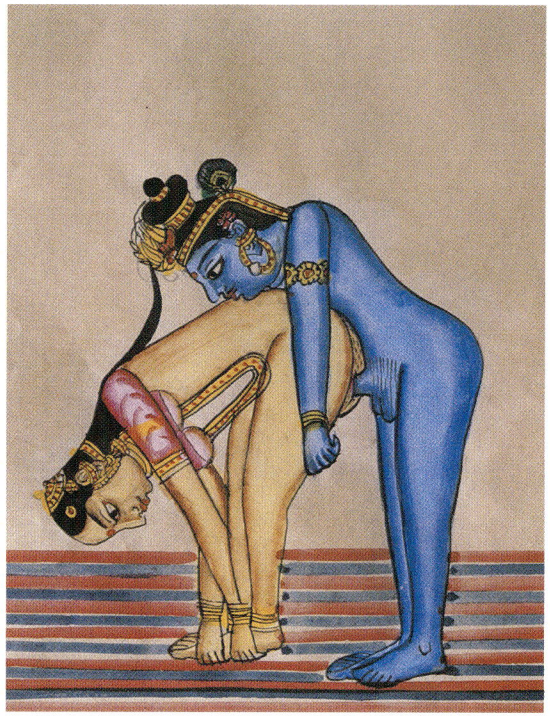

There are different types of coitus which enhance the sexual pleasure of lovers.

An ingenious person
Should multiply the kinds of coitus
After the fashion
Of different birds and beasts
For these different kinds of coitus
Performed according to the usage
Of each country
And each individual
Generate love, friendship, and respect
In the hearts of lovers.

On striking and sounds

There are sado-masochistic practices — including the use of instruments — prevalent in some places that would seem to belong in this chapter, but they are painful, barbarious, base, and quite unworthy of imitation. In the same vein, local peculiarities should not be adopted elsewhere, and even where prevalent, excess should always be avoided.

Love taps, on the other hand, are quite common everywhere as an embellishment to courting and coitus. A good example may be with the woman seated face-to-face in the man's lap, pretending to fight and hammering the soft sides of her fists against his chest. Another good example is when a man gently pats his lover's buttocks on any occasion. Vatsyayana links up these sidelights in the gentleness of love in his observation that coitus 'can be compared to a quarrel, on account of the contrariness of love and its tendency to dispute'.

As these are not meant to be violent actions, one may strike one's lover with the back of the hand, with the fingers a bit contracted (as when knocking), with the fist (preferably not as in boxing!), and with an open hand. With these one may strike the lover's shoulders, head, back, middle portion, sides, and between the breasts. On account of the marginal pain that may sometimes be caused, it is good to make some sound with each love tap, so that a loving intent is also clearly communicated; for example, one may cluck, growl, make funny or kissing sounds, and transparently pretend to quarrel. On the other hand, the lover must respond with some positive signals, and one must be particularly sensitive to any sound that may indicate prohibition, sufficiency, and a desire for liberation.

About such things
There can be no enumeration
Or definite rule;
Coitus having commenced
Passion alone gives birth
To all acts of the lovers.

Facing page and above: *A man acquainted with love knows his own strength, as well as the strength, impetuosity and tenderness of his lover.*

During coitus, and particularly towards climax, both lovers may involuntarily be a bit rough and make various sounds. For example, the woman may whimper, groan, make mewing sounds, and dig her nails into the man's back, and he in turn may press and squeeze her breasts, stomach, and waist, groan as if under tremendous strain, and finally let out rasping gasps of air as he climaxes.

The characteristics of manhood
Are said to consist

Of roughness and impetuosity.
While weakness, tenderness, sensibility
And an inclination to turn away
From unpleasant things
Distinguish womanhood.

The excitement of passion
And peculiarities of habit
May sometimes cause contrary characteristics to appear
But these do not last long
And in the end
The natural state is resumed.

The passionate actions, amorous gesticulations and movements of coitus cannot be defined, for they are as irregular as dreams. A horse in the fifth degree of motion goes on with blind speed, regardless of pits, ditches and posts in his way. In the same way, a loving pair become blind with passion in the heat of coitus, and both may go on impetuously, paying little regard to excess. This is why a man acquainted with the science and arts of love will know his strength as also the strength, impetuosity and tenderness of his lover, and always act accordingly. The various modes of sexual enjoyment are not for all times or all persons, but should each be used only at appropriate times, and only wherever it is acceptable. In doing or not doing so lie the means to gain renown, disdain, or even disrepute.

On the work of a man, and on women acting the part of a man

In love and coitus, whatever is done by a man to give pleasure to the woman, is called the 'work of a man'.

When a woman lies on your bed, abstracted by conversation, touches and blandishments, loosen the fastenings of her clothes and undergarments, and when she

protests, overwhelm her with kisses. Then, when your phallus is erect, press it against her with your whole body, and stroke, squeeze, and caress parts of her body with your hands and lips. If the woman is experienced but bashful, and if it is your first time together, put a hand between her thighs — which she will probably keep close together. If she is young and inexperienced, gently endeavour to get a hand under her breasts — which she will probably cover with her hands. Then twine your fingers through her hair, and hold her chin with your other hand to kiss her deeply (don't worry if she closes her eyes). If the woman is seasoned, do whatever is fitting to the occasion and agreeable to both of you. Throughout all of this, stay constantly aware of your lover's responses to everything you do, so as to find out what will be pleasing to her during coitus.

To this, Suvarnanabha adds that while a man does to a woman what he likes best in coitus, he should always make a point of pressing and caressing those parts of her body on which she turns her eyes.

Lovers may become blind with passion during lovemaking and may pay no heed to excesses.

Facing page: *The passionate actions, amorous gestures and movements of lovemaking cannot be defined because they are as irregular as dreams.*

The signs of a woman's enjoyment and satisfaction in coitus are that her body relaxes, she closes her eyes, abandons bashfulness, and shows a willingness for the man to thrust his phallus deeply into her vagina. The signs of lack of enjoyment and satisfaction are that she shakes her hands, does not let the man get up, feels dejected, bites, kicks, and continues to move after the man is finished. This is generally avoidable by more extended foreplay where the man also rubs his lover's vagina with his whole hand until it softens and grows humid and very moist, before inserting his phallus.

When a woman sees that her lover is exhausted from coitus, without having satisfied his desire, she should lay him on his back and assist him by assuming his role. She may also do so to satisfy her lover's curiosity or fancy, or even from her own desire for novelty (in any case, she can first ask him whether she may, to avoid seeming wanton).

The first way for a woman to assume the man's role in coitus is to turn around without breaking union, and the second way is to start afresh with the man on his back, straddled by the woman on her knees or on the balls of her feet. She should then smile, sigh, breathe heavily, press her breasts onto her lover's bosom, lower her head, and replicate his normal actions.. She may strike him, chaff him, and offer subtle clues to what she likes having done to herself, by her own actions. She may, for a bit of fun, declare that he had earlier laid her low with hard coitus, and that she will now do the same to him in return. At the end of coitus, she can again manifest her own bashfulness, her fatigue, and her desire to stop.

In sexual intercourse between a man and a woman, the positions assumed can only be limited by their imagination — nothing is taboo.

Coitus itself is essentially enacted with the man thrusting his phallus back and forth in his lover's vagina. He may just directly move his phallus backwards and forward; hold his phallus in his hand, and churn it around in her vagina; pierce the upper part of her vagina which peeps out just above the joint of her thighs when her legs are lowered together; he may rub his phallus against the base of her vagina when she raises it for him; press it deeply into her; 'give a blow' by withdrawing altogether and then thrusting back into her; repeatedly rub his phallus against just one part of her vagina in the 'boars blow', rub it alternately against both sides with the 'blow of the bull', and then finally move back and forth rapidly in the 'sporting of a sparrow', till climax.

Kama, lord of love and sensuality, seated on a horse composed of lovers.

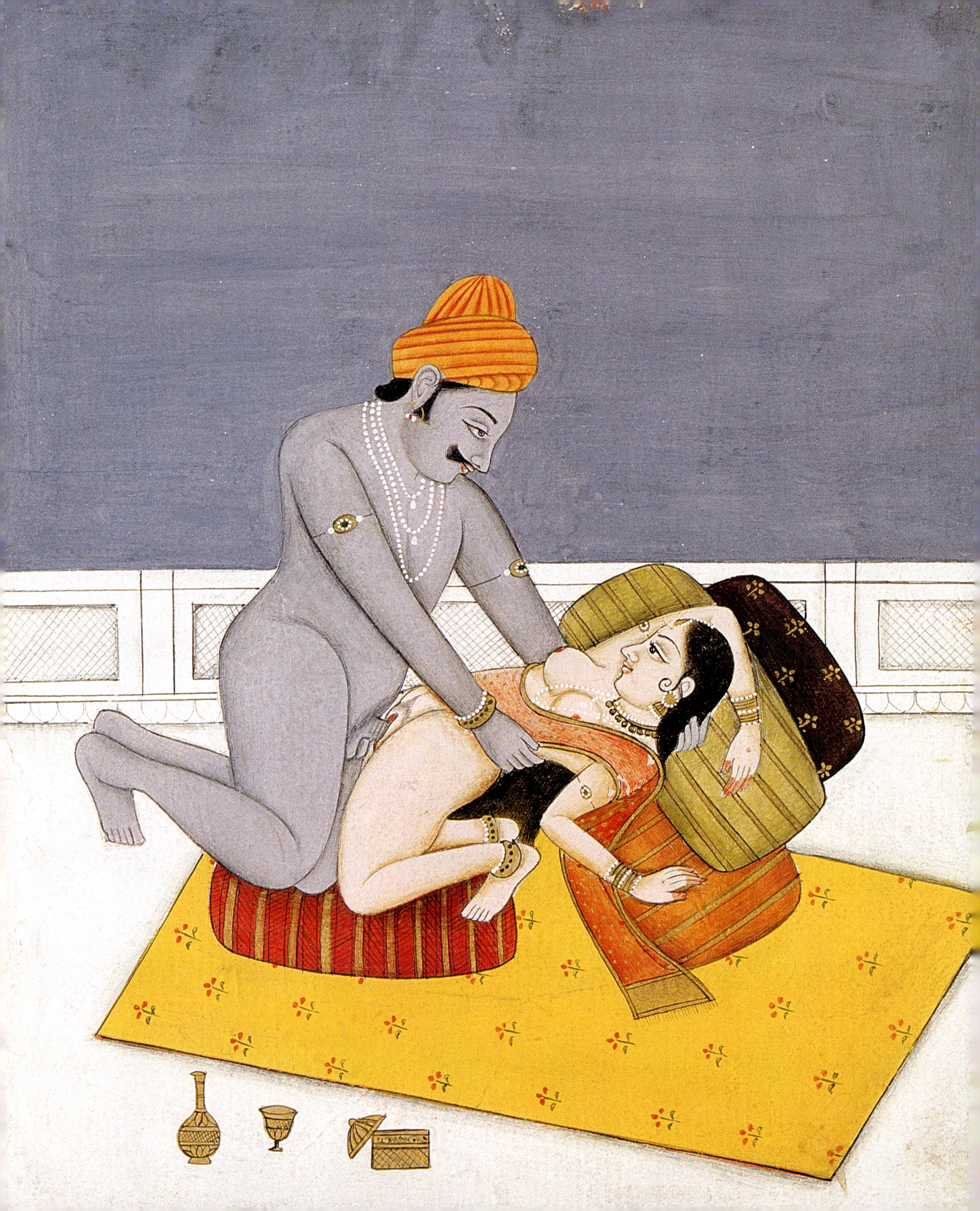

When a woman plays the man's role in coitus, she can do all this in addition to the following: hold, draw in, and press the man's phallus with her vagina; hold his phallus in her vagina and turn like a top with some practice, and, when his crotch is raised (with a cushion, or on his elbows and hands, for example), she can wrench his phallus about by grinding her own crotch around in circles against his, without releasing him. Finally, when the woman is exhausted from all this but neither are satiated, she should put her forehead to her lover's, rest without releasing his phallus, and then let him turn around to begin again.

Though a woman is reserved
And keeps her feelings concealed
Atop a man she shows
All her love and desire.

A man should gather
From the actions of a woman
Her disposition
And in what way
She likes to be enjoyed.

A woman having her periods
Or lately confined
And a fat woman
Should not
Be made to act
The part of a man.

Facing page and above: *If a man wishes to enslave a woman in erotic bondage, he should annoint his penis with a mixture of honey and powdered black pepper, long pepper and* datura.

If it be agreeable to both, either lover may orally serve the other in a sexual encounter, but of men performing on women, little more need be said than that the art of kissing the vagina is known from kissing the mouth. On the other hand, a woman performing on a man is a different matter, because it has no such parallel. Knowledge of the arts of *auparishtaka* is recommended to all women who wish to attempt it, so that they may guide each individual encounter entirely. It is best so, for a man thrusting his phallus into his lover's mouth in a sexual frenzy may easily choke her, bring up her bile,

There can be no definite rules for the art of making love. Once coitus commences, passion rules supreme.

and generally cause her to forever detest the experience. This is obviously, therefore, something that the man would also do well to remember.

The ideal way to go about it — for a woman intending to perform *auparishtaka* on her lover — is to begin when both lovers are just laying about or perhaps languidly massaging each other. The woman may run her hands all over the man's body to stir his passion, eventually arrive at his phallus when it is erect, and then playfully chaff him for getting into that state. If after this — even although he may have understood her intent — the man does not ask for *auparishtaka*, she may proceed anyway. On the other hand, if he demands it, she may dispute before grudgingly consenting, to maintain his respect for her, and perhaps to even tease his desire further.

There are eight basic steps that a woman should remember, for reference, in *auparishtaka*. In the sequence, she may pause after each step as if to stop — to make her lover ask for more — or go on directly to the next step anyway — if he does not:

1. She can hold her lover's phallus, and move her pursed lips over it for a 'nominal union'.

2. She can purse the length of her fingers over the end of his phallus like a flower bud, and bite the sides with lips and teeth.
3. She can apply pressure by putting her pursed lips against the tip of his phallus for a sucking kiss.
4. She can apply an inside pressure by taking his phallus into her mouth and then drawing it out between tightly compressed lips.
5. She can grip his phallus in her hands and apply pressure by kissing it passionately as she would her lover's lower lip.
6. She can rub his phallus all over with a licking tongue.
7. She can take his phallus half into her mouth, and forcibly suck it like a juicy mango.
8. She can swallow up her lover's phallus as if to devour it entirely.

During all this, the woman should also pay attention to the man's scrotum and testicles, lightly caressing them with her hands, softly scratching them with her nails and teeth, and perhaps even taking them entirely into her mouth to suck them gently; always keeping in mind that these are the most sensitive-to-pain parts of a man's entire body.

If either or both lovers are agreeable, they may orally serve each other in a sexual encounter.

Servile men
So serve their masters.

Some men
Knowing each other well
Also do so
Among themselves.
Some women among women
Act so
On each other vaginas
And some men
Also do so
To women.

Embraces should be such that those who ask, hear and talk about it are aroused. In coitus, embraces should increase love and passion.
Facing page: *When wooing a woman, a man should remember that all his conversation should be about love and not desire.*

When a man
And a woman
Do *auparishtaka* simultaneously
To each other
(With heads towards feet)
It is called
The 'coitus of a crow'.

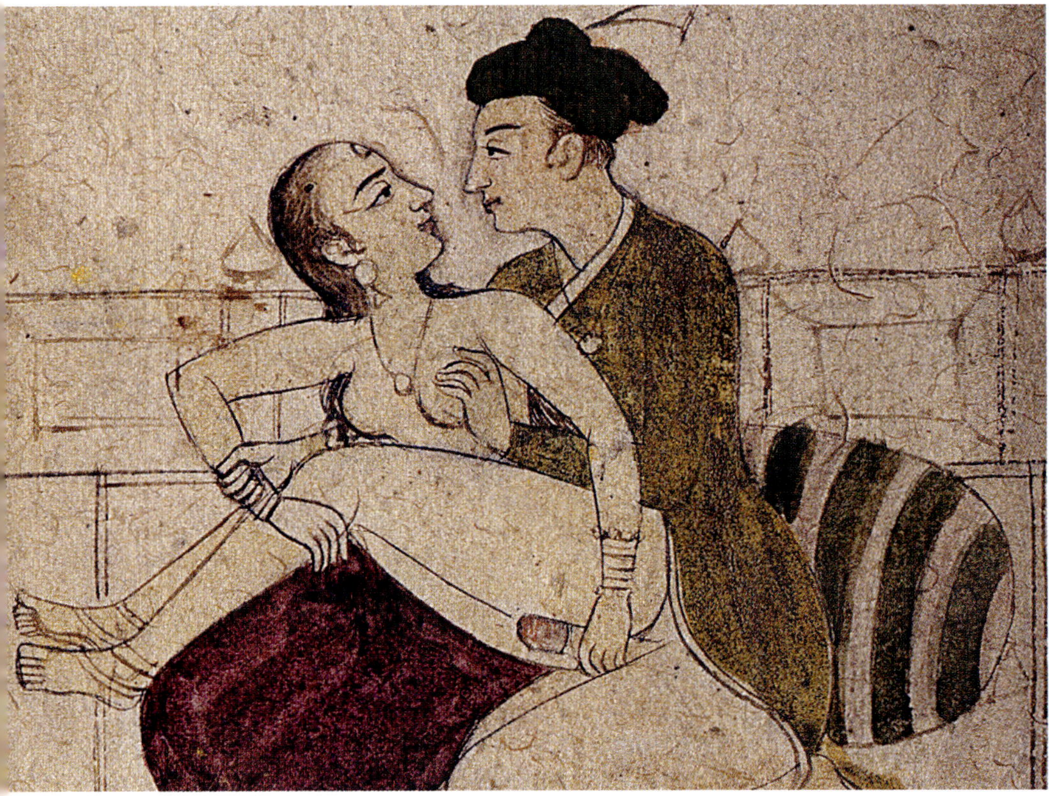

Promiscuous women may leave the finest of men for the basest, from a love of having *auparishtaka* done to them. Nevertheless, this is not recommended for a teacher, a minister who conducts the business of a state, or an eminent person of good reputation. On the other hand, there are some men, women, places and times, for which *auparishtaka* is always appropriate. One should therefore pay regard to place, time, and the practice intended, as also to whether it is agreeable to one's nature and oneself. Only then should

one practise *auparishtaka*. After all, these are your own secrets, and the minds of all men and women being unique, who can tell what any person will do at any particular time, or for any particular purpose?

On how to begin and how to end coitus, the different kinds of coitus, and on love quarrels

Before coitus, when a man seats his lover beside himself among friends of both sexes in a small and intimate social gathering, or in a completely private setting, he may touch her hair, clothes fastenings, dress and ornaments, and even bring around his hand from the side away from her to lightly embrace her. Both may allow the conversation to occasionally get a bit risque, but should also talk and debate on matters such as the arts and other such subjects; even sing, play or listen to music, and persuade each other to eat and drink. At last, when both lovers are filled with love and desire, they may proceed to coitus as earlier described, after first parting properly from the rest of the company.

❋

It is said that the man who employs the sixty-four sexual postures advocated by Babhravya, obtains the object of his desires, a woman who is excellent in every way.

After coitus, lovers should allow each other the small modesty of going separately out of the room for a wash. They should then settle down again as they were when they finished, nibble on something, and the man can perhaps massage his lover, paying attention to her marks and bruises, and also cuddle her. Some lovers may now like to eat or drink something light, something sweet, pure and gentle on the constitution. They can also sit on an open terrace or balcony, enjoy the moonlight, and just chat after coitus. The man may even lay his lover down with her head on his lap and her face to the moon, and point out to her the different constellations, the planets, and the stars.

Of coitus itself, there are several kinds:

1. When old lovers come together after awhile with difficulty, or when either has returned from a journey, or after making up after a quarrel and separation, a 'loving coitus' can be indulged in according to their mutual fancy, for as long as they choose.
2. When lovers come together in the infancy of their love, it is a 'coitus of subsequent love'.

3. When the man has to consciously excite himself in coitus, or when a couple comes together although each one loves another, in a 'coitus of artificial love', all the ways and means of the arts of love should be used.
4. Either or both lovers may enact a 'coitus of transferred love', by imagining the other to be someone else, during the course of the act.,
5. When a man takes advantage of an unfortunate or less-privileged woman to satisfy only his own desires, there are no kisses, loving touches or manipulations, in this 'coitus like a eunuch'.
6. 'Deceitful coitus' is indulged in with rustics, foreigners, tourists, and other transients.

❋

A man who is skilled in lovemaking is looked upon with love by his own wife and all other women.

7. When each lover loves the other and acts according to their mutual liking, there is beautiful 'spontaneous coitus'.

When a woman quarrels with a man from jealousy, he should use conciliatory words and gentleness to soothe her. She in turn may be a bit violent with him and then stand crying by the door leading out (Dattaka recommends that she should not actually go out as her lover may then find fault with her for having done so). After awhile, when s he thinks that her lover's conciliatory words and actions have reached the utmost, she may embrace him while still talking harshly and reproaching him, but should show a desire to have him make love to her. When a woman is in her own house, however, she may leave, and the man should send friends and messengers to pacify her. She should then accompany these people back, and spend the night with her lover.

A man employing the sixty-four means
Mentioned by Babhravya
Obtains his object
And enjoys
A woman
Of the first quality.
When ignorant of these sixty-four divisions
Though well spoken on other subjects
No great respect
Shall be paid
To such a man
In the assembly of the learned.
A man devoid of other knowledge
But well-versed in the sixty-four divisions
Becomes a leader

In any society
Of men
And women.

What man will not respect
Those sixty-four parts
That are respected by the learned
The cunning
And the courtesans?

As these sixty-four parts
Are respected
Are charming
And add to the talent
Of women
They are called
The sages dear to women.

A man skilled
In the sixty-four parts
Is looked upon with love
By his own wife
The wives of others
And all promiscuous women.

The sixty-four parts repeatedly mentioned in these verses was originally an ancient title for this chapter. Among the uninitiated, it has often been erroneously concluded from this that Vatsyayana's *Kamasutra* contains descriptions of sixty-four possible positions in coitus. The reader will see that this is far from true. Vatsyayana had in fact discussed the old title in his treatise, and had recommended that it be taken as just a convenient label for everything contained in all the ten parts of the entire chapter.

As far as coitus is concerned, one should pay regard to place, time and the practice intended.

33

A man wins the admiration of a woman by maintaining a fit and healthy physique, which should reflect a sound mind and strong feelings.

CHAPTER 3

ON MARRIAGE

By marriage to a chaste person who is not promiscuous, one acquires *dharma*, *artha*, offspring, appreciation, increase of friends, untarnished love, and a universally respectable partnership in the pursuit of *kama*. A man should therefore ideally fix his affection upon a girl of good family, who is at least three years younger than himself, possessed of some wealth, well connected, beautiful, and of good disposition. She should have a healthy body, which is well-proportioned. Needless to say, all of this also applies equally to men.

Ghotakamukha held that it is reproachable for one to love a girl who has already been joined to others. Some authors have, however, argued that there is true gain only in marriage to the girl whom one becomes attached to, and that therefore no girl other than the loved one should be married by anyone.

For such a marriage, have friends and relatives assist in winning over parents by all fair means. Exaggerated compliments may be paid, and faults may be diplomatically pointed out in one's rivals. One can also target the mother's friends, and enlist their help in causing her to become jealous of her offspring's rivals.

Ghotakamukha adds here that one should not indiscriminately get married without regard to signs. For example, a girl asleep, crying, betrothed already, or gone out of the house when sought in marriage, should not be married. According to Vatsyayana's recommendations, one should also avoid marriage to a girl who is kept concealed, or who has an ill-sounding name, a depressed nose, turned up nostrils, a body like a man, or one that is bent over, crooked thighs, a projecting forehead, a bald head, glandular enlargements, or a

Facing page: *Lord Krishna and Radha, his divine lover — who epitomise the quintessence of love between man and woman in its multi-faceted forms – surrounded by the* gopis.

serious disfigurement. One should also not marry a friend, a sister, a child or adolescent, a person whose palms and soles always perspire, one who dislikes purity, or one who has been sexually enjoyed by others.

When a girl becomes marriageable, her parents should dress her well, and have her socially seen to advantage. They should welcome and be gracious to suitors seeking their daughter's hand in marriage, but set a later date for decision, when asked directly the first time. Eventually, when a partner is won according to the customs of a country, or by one's own desire, marriage should ideally be conducted by the precepts of the prevailing holy writ.

Amusement in society
Should be
With neither superiors
Nor inferiors
But amongst equals.
That should be known
As a high connection.
When a man
After marrying a girl
Serves her and her
relatives like a servant
And such a connection
Is censured by the good.
The wise know
A low connection
When a man and his
relatives
Lord it over his wife.
But when both afford
Mutual pleasure

When a girl is of marriageable age, her parents should dress her well and ensure that she is socially seen to advantage.

To each other
And relatives on both sides
Pay respect to one another
It is a connection
In the proper sense of the word.
Therefore a man
Should not contract
A high connection
By which he is obliged
To bow down afterwards
To his kinsmen;

Nor a low connection
Which is universally reprehensible to all.

On creating confidence and winning over the girl

There are many prescriptions for the first days of marriage in every society, but Vatsyayana recommends that a man should first win over the girl, create confidence in her, and only then progress to sexual pleasures. Women are of a tender nature and desire tender beginnings. When approached forcibly by a man, a woman may suddenly begin to hate all sexual intercourse, and even all men.

With this in mind, a man should first approach his lady according to her liking, and do everything to establish himself in her confidence. Short embraces should be well received early in a relationship, but it may help to do so in the dark if the girl is young and inexperienced. Offer trifles to eat, and kiss her softly and gracefully on the mouth without a sound. Prompt her to talk, with questions requiring short answers. Don't frighten her if she does not speak, but continue in a conciliatory manner. Ghotakamukha observed that 'all girls hear everything said to them by men, but do not themselves sometimes say a single word'. It is therefore often nice to have a female friend of the man join in the verbal sparring during early courtship in a marriage.

In the beginning of a relationship, a man can gently unsettle a girl by dragging a fingernail across her skin, and if she tries to prevent him from doing so, he can humorously negotiate that she must embrace him to have him stop. Then, in the embrace he can move his hands about her body. He can even jestingly hold her on his lap and tease her that he will mark her breasts with his teeth and nails, mark himself, and then declare to all

that she has done it. By such and other ways — just as fear and confidence is created in the minds of children — a man can gradually win a young wife over to his wishes.

On perhaps the second or third night, after the girl's confidence has increased somewhat, the man can feel her whole body with his hands while both are still dressed, and also kiss her all over. He should then massage her thighs and her crotch through her clothes, gently persuading her to let him do so if she resists, by asking her what harm there is in it. Only then should he proceed to touch her private parts, loosen her clothes, massage her naked crotch, and do other things by various pretences while still not attempting coitus. He should then begin to teach her about sexual matters, tell her of his love, describe the hopes he entertained regarding her, promise fidelity, and dispel whatever fears she may still have. At last, after overcoming her bashfulness, the man may begin to sexually enjoy the girl, always taking care never to frighten her.

A man should seek to gain
A girl's love and confidence
By acting according to her inclinations.
A man should seek a middle course
For he shall not succeed
By implicitly following a girl's inclinations
Or by wholly opposing her.
He who increases her honour
And creates confidence in her
Becomes the object
Of a girl's love.
He who neglects a girl
Thinking her to be too bashful
Is despised by her as a beast
Ignorant of the workings
Of a woman's mind.
Moreover a girl forcibly enjoyed
By one who does not understand
The hearts of girls
Becomes nervous, uneasy, dejected
And suddenly begins to hate
The man who has taken advantage of her;
And when her love

A house should be well appointed with every possible comfort, such as comfortable couches and chairs, swings, hammocks, some open space, and a garden.
Facing page: *During the first days of marriage, a man should first win over the girl, gain her confidence, and then only make sexual overtures.*

❋

A man should seek to gain a woman's love and respect by finding out her inclination and acting accordingly. This will make him the object of her love.

Is neither understood nor returned
She sinks into despondency
And becomes a hater of all men
Or, hating her own man alone
Will have recourse to other men.

On courtship and manifestation of feelings by outward signs and deeds; and on how to win the favours of the person one desires

A man who has perceived
The inclination of a girl towards him
Having noticed
The outward signs and movements
By which these feelings are expressed
Should do everything in his power
To effect a union with her:
He should gain over a young girl
By childlike sports
A damsel of age
By his skills in the arts
And a girl who loves him
By having recourse
To the persons in whom she confides.

According to Vatsyayana, women, when approached at proper times in proper places, do not turn away from their lovers.

Ancient sages, however, held that although a maid may love a man ever so much, she should not offer herself or make the first overtures, for a girl who does this loses her dignity, and is liable to be exploited, or scorned and rejected. When the man shows his desire for her, she should favour him, but receive all manifestations of his love as though ignorant of his state of mind. When he tries to kiss her, she should delicately oppose him; when he begs for coitus she should let him touch her private parts only, and that too with considerable difficulty; when importuned by the man, she should still never yield herself as if of her own accord. Only when completely certain of his total devotion and true love, and when sure he will not be inconstant, should a girl then give herself up to her lover, and persuade him to have an early marriage. Upon thus losing her virginity, a girl should tell her closest friends about it.

A girl much sought after
Should marry of her choice
The man who will respect her

A wise and ingenious man is always accompanied by a friend. He knows well the intentions of others, and also that there is a proper time and place for everything. Such a man can win the favours of even a woman who is difficult to please.

And give her pleasure.
When married off for wealth
By her parents
She will never be attached to the man
Regardless of his qualities.

A respectful husband
Obedient, yet master of himself
Though he be poor and not good looking
Is better than one common to many women
Though he be handsome and attractive.
The wives of rich men
Who have many women
Are never greatly attached to them
Never confidential with them
And even though possessed
Of all the external enjoyments of life
Often still have recourse
To other men.
A man of low mind
Fallen from his social position
And given much to travel
Does not deserve to be married;
Neither does a man with a history
Of many women and children;
Or one who comes to his wife
Only when he pleases.

When a man is trying to seduce a woman, his attention must be concentrated on her. He must not attempt to carry on another seduction at the same time.

Of all the lovers of a girl
He alone is her true husband
Who possesses the qualities liked by her
And such a husband enjoys
Real superiority over her
Only because
He is the husband of love.

On certain forms of marriage

When a girl is won over and behaves openly with the man as his wife, some coercion is allowed by ancient texts in marrying her, if she cannot decide and will not express readiness (this may not, however, be acceptable in many modern societies). In this Gandharva form of marriage, parents may be informed after the event, and relatives should be gradually acquainted with the matter in ways that will ensure their consent and approval, overlooking the manner in which it was all brought about. All should eventually be reconciled by favourable conduct.

In all forms of marriage by coercion
The lesser coercion shall be the better
On account of being less against
The commands of religion.
As the fruit of all good marriages is love
When it fulfils this object
The Gandharva form of marriage is respected
Even though formed
Under unfavourable circumstances.
It is also respected
Because it brings forth happiness
Causes less trouble in its performance
Than the other forms of marriage
And is above all
The result of previous love.

There are innumerable instances of men and women making love in the open — in paintings and sculpture. The settings are as varied as jungles, gardens, picnic spots, terraces and balconies.

Page 81: *In the early days of marriage, a man can hold his young wife on his lap, in jest. He can tease her by threatening to mark her breasts with his teeth and nails, then mark himself, and tell everyone that she has done it.*

CHAPTER 4

ON THE BEHAVIOUR OF A VIRTUOUS WIFE

A virtuous woman who loves her husband will respect him, and the gods and persons he worships and respects. She will participate in the everyday maintenance of his household, and behave towards his parents, relations, friends and servants as they deserve. In planning meals she will consider her husband's likes and dislikes, in addition to what is good and what is bad for him. She will spend some time attending to his needs when he returns home, dress well when going out with him, always consult him when accepting or issuing invitations, and never discuss his financial affairs with others.

When her husband finds fault with her in any matter, the virtuous wife will not blame him excessively or use harsh and abusive language, but will instead show some displeasure and rebuke him adequately in conciliatory words. She will never scold and be sharp-tongued, for Gonardiya made it clear that 'there is no cause for dislike on the part of a husband so great as this characteristic in a wife'.

The virtuous wife will avoid bad expressions, sulky looks, speaking under her breath, standing always in the doorway, looking at passersby, socialising excessively, and remaining in lonely places for long periods of time. She will keep herself clean, dress simply in

Facing page: *Only after a girl has overcome her bashfulness should a man have sexual relations with her. He should be careful never to frighten her.*

A virtuous wife participates in the maintenance of the household, always behaving with her husband's family, relatives, friends and servants with amiability and courtesy.

the normal course with no more than a bit of perfume, and will not be vain and always taken up by her own enjoyments. She will dress up well just for her husband, and occasionally make at least nominally sacrificial gestures for him.

When her husband is away, the virtuous wife will be a bit more austere in her lifestyle than normal, to preserve her reputation and her husband's dignity.

The wife
Whether of noble
Lascivious
Or disadvantaged
background
Should lead a chaste live
Devoted to her husband
And committed to his
welfare.

Women thus acquire
dharma, *artha*, and
kama
Obtain a high position
And keep husbands
Devoted to them.

A good wife always considers her husband's likes and dislikes, and also what is good and what is bad for him — in planning meals, arranging the house, in her dressing, and so forth.

*

When her husband returns home, a loving and dutiful wife should spend some time with him, attending to his needs. She should dress well when going out with him and always consult him when accepting and issuing invitations.

CHAPTER 5

ON CHARACTERISTICS OF MEN AND WOMEN

The wives of other men may be approached for sexual pleasures on the occasions already described in Chapter 1, but the possibility of gaining one over, her fitness for cohabitation, the danger to oneself in uniting with her, and the future effect of such a union should all be first considered. A man may also approach the wife of another when he finds that his love for her proceeds from one degree to another, threatening to eventually destroy him if it remains unfulfilled.

Some ancient sages held that a man can know the disposition, truthfulness, purity and will of a young woman, as also the intensity or weakness of her passions, from the form of her body, and from her characteristic marks and signs. Vatsyayana contested this and opined that these are but erring tests of character, and that women should instead be judged by their conduct, the outward expression of their thoughts, and by the movements of their bodies. Gonikaputra in turn laid down as a general rule that women at least momentarily fall in love with every handsome man they see, and so do all men with a beautiful woman, but rarely is this ever carried forward.

Women in love are often difficult to understand. They can love without regard for what may be right or wrong, and often do not consciously seek to win the man they desire for any particular purpose. They may therefore shrink from the man's first sexual overtures, even when they are actually quite willing, and so men should always repeatedly try to gain them over.

When a woman seeks to win over a man, and he has perhaps even begun to love her, a regard for morality and wisdom may constrain him from ever yielding. On the other hand,

Whatever a woman's background, she should lead a chaste life, devoted to her husband and totally committed to his welfare. In this way, women acquire dharma, artha *and* kama, *and keep their husbands devoted to them.*

sometimes after failing to win a woman, the man may suddenly leave the whole matter to be dealt with at some future time. In the same way, men are often known to grow indifferent to a woman after they have won her. As for the saying that a man cares not for what is easily gained, and desires only that which can be gained with difficulty, is only a matter of talk.

When a man recognises that a woman is rejecting his advances for any of the following reasons, he should endeavour to remove the cause at the very beginning of his courtship, where it is possible and not improper:

1. The woman may have a healthy affection for her husband.
2. She may have a desire for legitimate progeny.
3. She may lack opportunity.

4. She may be angered at the man's overfamiliarity.
5. She may be affected by a difference in social standing.
6. She may lack confidence because the man is often away.
7. She may think the man is already committed elsewhere.
8. She may fear that the man will not keep their secret.
9. She may think the man is too devoted to his friends.
10. She may apprehend lack of earnestness.
11. She may be bashful because of his eminence in society.
12. She may fear the power of his sexual drives and passion, or even just the imagined size of his phallus.
13. She may be in awe of his intelligence.
14. She may be affected by having lived with him as a friend.

When her husband finds fault with her and chides her regarding any matter, a virtuous wife will not retaliate with harsh words. Instead, she will show her displeasure mildly, and rebuke him with love.

15. She may have contempt for his intellect.
16. She may distrust his low character.
17. She may be disgusted by his not recognising her love for him.
18. She may think him to be sexually inadequate for her pleasure.
19. She may fear for him.
20. She may think herself to be inferior to him.
21. She may fear discovery.
22. She may be disillusioned by his age or appearance.
23. She may fear that he is her husband's agent.
24. She may think him to be too committed to morality.

The following are kinds of men who will generally be successful in winning over women:

1. Men who are skilled in courtship and the arts of love.
2. Men who are skilled in storytelling.
3. Men who have always been among women from childhood.
4. Men who quickly secure the confidence of women.
5. Men who send women presents.
6. Men who converse well.
7. Men who are used to doing what they please.
8. Men who have not loved other women previously.
9. Men who act as messengers for friends.
10. Men who know the weak points of women.
11. Men who are desired by other good women.
12. Men who are already lovers of the woman's friends.
13. Men who are goodlooking.
14. Men who have been brought up with the woman.
15. Men who are the woman's neighbours.
16. Men who are ardently devoted to sexual pleasures.
17. Men who have been lovers of the daughter of the woman's nurse.
18. Men who have been recently married.
19. Men who like picnics and parties.
20. Men who are liberal.
21. Men who are celebrated for their sexual prowess.
22. Men who are enterprising and brave.

Women in love are sometimes difficult to understand. They can love without considering what is right or wrong, and often do not consciously seek to win a man they desire. They may shrink from a man's overtures, even though they may be quite willing.

Pages 92-93: *A virtuous wife should dress simply, with no more than a little perfume — only for her husband should she dress well. She should not be vain and always preoccupied with her own enjoyment. Occasionally, she should make even some nominal sacrifices for him.*

There is much in common between the relationship between friends and that between lovers. It is the lovers' joint pursuit of pleasure, and the uniquely exciting adventure that is their lovemaking, that differentiates the two.

23. Men who surpass the woman's husband in good qualities and liberality.
24. Men who are magnificent in dress and lifestyle.

The following are the kinds of women who may easily be gained over by men for just sexual pleasures:

1. A woman who often stands at the doorway of her house.
2. A woman who is always looking out on the street.
3. A woman who is always gossiping in her neighbour's house.
4. A woman who is always staring at you when you are together.
5. A woman who acts as a messenger.
6. A woman who casts sideward glances at you when you are together.
7. A woman who lost her husband to another woman without just cause.
8. A woman who hates and is hated by her own husband.
9. A woman who has no one to care for her or keep her in check.

10. A woman who has had no children.
11. A woman whose background is not well known.
12. A woman whose children have died.
13. A woman who is overfond of socialising.
14. A woman who is overdemonstrative in her affection for her husband.
15. The wife of an actor
16. A widow
17. A poor woman
18. A woman too fond of enjoyment
19. The wife of a man with many younger brothers
20. A vain woman
21. A woman married to a man inferior to herself in various ways.
22. A woman who is too proud of her abilities.
23. A woman who is disturbed in the mind about her husband's folly.
24. A woman who was married when she was too young, who has grown up to find her husband not suited to her tastes.
25. A woman who has been slighted by her husband without cause.
26. A woman who is not respected by her female equals.

Men who can easily secure the confidence of women, and those who converse well — such men are successful in winning the hearts of women.

27. A woman whose husband is devoted to travelling.
28. The wife of a jeweller
29. A jealous woman
30. A covetous woman
31. An immoral woman
32. A barren woman
33. A lazy woman
34. A cowardly woman
35. A physically disadvantaged woman

Desire which springs naturally
And which is increased by art
And from which
Danger is removed by wisdom
Is firm and secure.

On getting acquainted with a woman and on efforts to gain her over

Vatsyayana made it clear that a man should always be himself when making the acquaintance and trying to win a woman, unless it is clearly impractical or impossible. Other writers agreed but insisted that the wives of other men are always best approached by a go-between.

A man should first arrange to meet the woman he desires in a public or social gathering where he can communicate his state of mind by the way he looks at her. He should talk about her and other women with his friends when she looks at him, somehow demonstrate his liberality and appreciation of enjoyment, and talk pleasantly to her about some third person, such as a child. He should then use this first meeting to visit her, and establish a relationship by putting something in her charge, or even by introducing her to his own wife and encouraging a friendship. He should develop some joint interests with the woman that allow him to pay her long visits, ideally on the pretence of some business that will have each visit lead to another. He should show a willingness to place himself at her disposal within his abilities and powers, without seeming slavish, talk to her openly in company, and always make a point of behaving as her guardian of the moment when they are together. Only when this friendship has progressed well should a man make an effort to win the woman over sexually.

A man who is interested in a woman should discover some joint interests, which will allow him to pay her long visits.

Facing page: *A good wife will always have a pleasant expression on her face; not stand in the doorway, looking at passersby; nor socialise excessively.*

Girls are not well acquainted with sexual matters, so a man should proceed cautiously and with the greatest delicacy when dealing with them, but if a woman is experienced, the man may be much more straightforward with her. When some reciprocal intent in the woman becomes clear and bashfulness is set aside, he should develop a more intimate relationship by borrowing her things and even gifting her subtly erotic gifts — such as a single flower marked by his teeth and nails. He should work to dispel whatever remaining fears and reservations she may still have, and by degrees get her to a place where he can embrace and kiss her. When he is eventually able to touch her private parts, the entire effort has been drawn to a satisfactory conclusion with a sexual liaison initiated.

A wise man will not attempt to seduce more than one woman at a time. He will first win one, enjoy her for a good length of time, win her affection, and only then begin the seduction of another. He will never join with a woman when her husband is not far away, and he will not even think of seducing a woman who is apprehensive, timid, untrustworthy, well guarded, or living with her in-laws.

On understanding the state of a woman's mind

When attempting to win over a woman, a man must continuously remain aware of her state of mind.

If a woman accepts a man's advances without responding or offering any clue to her intentions, he needs to use a go-between. If, after the first meeting she tries to improve her appearance for the next visit, or agrees to meet in a lonely place, she will easily be won. If she accepts the courtship

According to ancient sages, a man can discover the disposition of a woman (whether she is truthful and chaste), and also the intensity or weakness of her passions, from the shape of her body and her characteristic marks and signs.

but will not yield even after a long time, she is a simple flirt, but may still be won over by continuing a close acquaintance. When she avoids the man's courtship due to her respect for him or pride in herself, she will be won only with great difficulty, by maintaining familiarity for a long while, or with the help of a very clever go-between. If she responds to the courtship with harsh words, the effort should immediately be abandoned. When she is teasingly reproachful of the man's advances, he will have to use all his arts to win her. When she pretends unawareness of the man's casual touches, due to indecision, he should continue his courtship with patience and extra effort.

When a woman is falsely and coyly reproachful regarding a man's advances, he should use all his guiles and arts to win her.

When a man believes that his courtship of a woman is progressing well, he should test this by casually putting an arm around her shoulders at some time. If the woman moves away but is as usual the next day, she is not unwilling. If she avoids the man for a while, he should use a go-between, but if she avoids him for a while and then returns and is as always, she will not object. When the woman gives opportunities to the man and clearly manifests a love for him, he can proceed to enjoy her.

A woman may manifest her affection for a man in various ways:

1. She may call him before he calls her.
2. She may give him opportunities to meet her in private.
3. She may speak tremblingly and inarticulately to him.
4. Her face may bloom with delight and her hands may perspire when she is with him.
5. She may touch him in various seemingly innocent ways.
6. She may hold his hand or sleeve, etc., often, as if unconsciously.
7. She may put her head on his lap and be willing to massage him or be massaged by him.
8. She may allow him to squeeze her hand, press parts of her body, and even let him put his hand between her thighs.
9. She may be back the next day after having resisted his efforts to win her.

When a woman gives no encouragement to a man's courtship, but does not avoid him either, he should approach her simultaneously through one of her female confidants. If after this she is still the same, he will need a very skilled go-between. If she still has nothing to say to the man, he should consider well before making any further attempt to win her.

The sequence in courtship that emerges from all this is that a man should first obtain an introduction to the woman he desires, develop a friendship, and somehow hint at his love for her. If this is well received and encouraged, he should work to fully win her over. A woman who clearly demonstrates love by her behaviour towards the man at the first meeting, will be easily won. A woman who frankly responds to the man's courtship with words of love, may be considered to have been won over at that very moment. In fact, a rule may be laid down that any woman who makes some open manifestation of her love for a man will be easily won over by that man.

The business of a go-between

If a woman you desire has manifested reciprocal love or desire for you but you have not seen her since then, or if you desire a woman you have met for the first time, you may need a go-between to help you approach her. Gonikaputra adds here that if the woman seems inexperienced or has manifested her love very subtly, then you should choose someone already close to her to act as your go-between.

A good go-between will wheedle himself, or herself, into the confidence of the woman you desire, according to her disposition; telling tales, flattering her, always subtly putting down her husband or lover, and even frankly suggesting a sexual mismatch with that person, if it is at all possible to do so. The go-between will often talk of epic sexual escapades of goddesses and eminent women to allay any qualms the woman may have, and will read her response so as to be very clear about her disposition.

When a woman is favourable to the mission of a go-between, she will be welcoming and questioning. She will develop a close relationship with the go-between, invite him or her back, express a desire to meet again, and speak jestingly about the whole business to keep the topic alive. She will worriedly discuss the ramifications of yielding, and will enjoy being asked about anything that may have transpired directly between her and the person the go-between represents. She will often laugh at the man's desire for her, but will not be reproachful.

Women also have strong sexual drives. While men give in to and fulfil their desires, women derive pleasure from a consciousness of theirs. **Facing page:** Kama *must be learned by all because pleasure is as necessary as food for one's well being.*

When the woman's desire or interest is evident, the go-between will encourage an exchange of letters and presents, and eventually offer a personal guarantee of security to arrange a quiet meeting.

Auddalaka cautioned that using a go-between is pointless when the two people have not already met, or when they have never shown each other any affection. Babhravya clarified that a go-between is still useful when the two parties are unacquainted, but have nevertheless shown each other signs of possible affection. Gonikaputra then added that a go-between is also useful when the two people are acquainted with each other but have never shown any signs of mutual affection. Vatsyayana finally laid down that when the two parties are unacquainted and have also never shown each other signs of affection, both may still wish to independently put their faith in the hands of a good go-between.

The other writers on *kama* also spoke of various appropriate places for the first

meeting, contrived by a go-between, but Vatsyayana laid down that it should be set for a place with proper means of entry and exit, where arrangements can be made so that no disagreeable encounter or accidental occurrence will mar the occasion when the potential lovers arrive, spend time together, and eventually leave.

There are various kinds of go-betweens, for example:

1. One who takes on the total responsibility for the affair.
2. One who just helps things along after some progress has already been made.
3. One who just carries messages and letters.
4. One who acts for himself or herself, whether by original intent or subsequent desire.
5. One who assists an innocent young wife in winning over and getting along with her husband.
6. A lover, wife, or husband may also act as a go-between.
7. A go-between may also act purely on instruction.
8. A person may also be unwittingly used as a go-between without ever understanding the function they serve.

It has been said that a good go-between can unite a man and woman even when such an event may seem unlikely, by sheer artfulness of conversation. A good go-between can also bring together a man and woman who have earlier separated from each other for some reason.

Women love men who are skilled in courtship and in the arts of lovemaking.
Facing page: *When united with a lover, delight him with the application of tender means of enjoyment.*

On the love of powerful men for the wives of others

There are ways and means
Employed in different countries
By men of power
To seduce the wives of others.
But a virtuous and good man
Of power
Will never put them
Into practice.
A great man

Who has conquered
The six enemies of mankind
Namely lust, anger, avarice
Spiritual ignorance
Pride and envy
Becomes the master
Of the whole earth
And of himself.

On promiscuous wives

Women have sexual drives of their own, and may allay their passions in a variety of ways, for a variety of reasons. The most damaging of these ways, to the psyche of a man, is when his woman turns to another man. History and everyday reality offers innumerable examples of this, and while one may believe that such is the behaviour of the wives of others, this should serve as a warning for all men to take care of their own.

As a precaution, Babhravya recommended that a man should allow his wife to associate with a woman who will learn her secrets and reveal them to the man, but Vatsyayana wisely counselled that no good can be derived from having one's wife associate with such a deceitful woman.

Among the many reasons that may contribute to the promiscuity of a wife, are the following:

1. She may be always socialising.
2. She may have a straightforward absence of restraint.
3. She may be reacting to her husband's loose habits.

Babhravya suggested that a deceitful wife should be allowed to associate with another woman, who will discover her secrets and reveal them to her husband.

A clever man, adept at winning over the wives of others, is never deceived in the case of his own.

4. There may be a want of caution in her relations with other men.
5. She may be responding to the continued and long absences of her husband.
6. She may be affected by the culture shock of living in a new country.
7. Her husband may have destroyed her love for him.
8. She may be keeping the company of loose women.
9. She may be influenced by her husband's jealousy.

A clever man
Learning from the Shastras
The ways of winning over
The wives of others
Is never deceived
In the case of his own.
No one, however,
Should make use of these ways
For seducing
The wives of others
Because they do not always succeed
And often cause disaster and destruction
Of *dharma* and *artha*.
This book is intended
For the good of people
And to teach them
The ways of keeping their own wives
And should not be used
Merely for gaining over
The wives of others.

CHAPTER 6

ON COURTESANS

Vatsyayana described courtesans as women whose union with men is ruled solely by their own desire for wealth, freedom from misfortune, and love. Accordingly, by intercourse with men, courtesans seek both pleasure and their own maintenance. Given that this may seem contradictory, in so far as taking up with a man for love is natural, while doing so for money is artificial or even forced, a clever courtesan will at least feign love to gain the confidence of a man. She will never demonstrate avarice and always avoid taking money by unlawful means from any man. She will show herself in society, and form friendships with people who can help her repair her misfortunes, acquire wealth, win the men she desires, and protect her from being bullied by people with whom she interacts.

The best men for courtesans are those of privileged birth, learned, worldly-wise, eloquent, energetic, multi-talented, foresighted, persevering, devoted, liberal, sociable, affectionate, powerful in sexual enjoyment, and free from anger, envy and suspicion. They should be healthy, have good bodies and independent means of livelihood, avoid alcoholism, be always aware of the appropriateness of time and place, and have a talent for winning over women, without ever being entirely devoted to them.

The basic qualities of all good women are that they should be intelligent, have a good disposition and manners, be straightforward, know how to be grateful, and always consider the consequences of all their actions. They should be active,

Facing page: *There are many reasons which could lead to a woman becoming promiscuous — she may be always socialising or may keep the company of loose women.*

consistent in their behaviour, act appropriately according to time and place, and will always speak without meanness, loud laughter, malignity, anger, dullness or stupidity. Lastly, all good women should have a positive attitude towards coitus with their lovers, and develop and maintain at least some sexual skills.

The additional basic qualities of all good courtesans are that they should be beautiful and have good bodies; they should appreciate good qualities in others, enjoy wealth, love sex with men who love them, and have firm minds with lusts and a sexual drive as strong as any man's; they should always be anxious to acquire experience and knowledge, enjoy society and the arts, and never demonstrate avarice.

Good courtesans should never sacrifice money for love, for wealth should be their main objective. In case of fear, however, they should act according to the compulsions of the circumstances. They should never be easily won over and should always find out more about men who make advances to them, from friends, to discover what may be the person's true feelings and state of mind, whether his feelings are pure or impure, affected or unaffected, and whether the man is capable of attachment or is indifferent, liberal or niggardly. If after all this a courtesan finds a man to her liking, she should have appropriate people help her fix the man's affection fully on her.

When a courtesan is ready to directly win over a man, she should have a confidant bring him to her house or visit him herself, on any pretence. She should give him a present for his personal use that will arouse curiosity and love in his heart, and amuse him with stories and by doing things he delights in. When he is away, she should visit him on the pretence of some business, and frequently send him small presents through a female attendant, who can also amuse him.

When a lover comes
Serve him well
Show skill in the arts and entertain him
With long conversations
Give him loving presents

Below and facing page: *According to Vatsyayana, courtesans are women whose relationships with men are always ruled by their own desire for wealth, freedom from misfortune, and for love. Therefore, in their interaction with men, they seek both pleasure and the means to maintain themselves.*

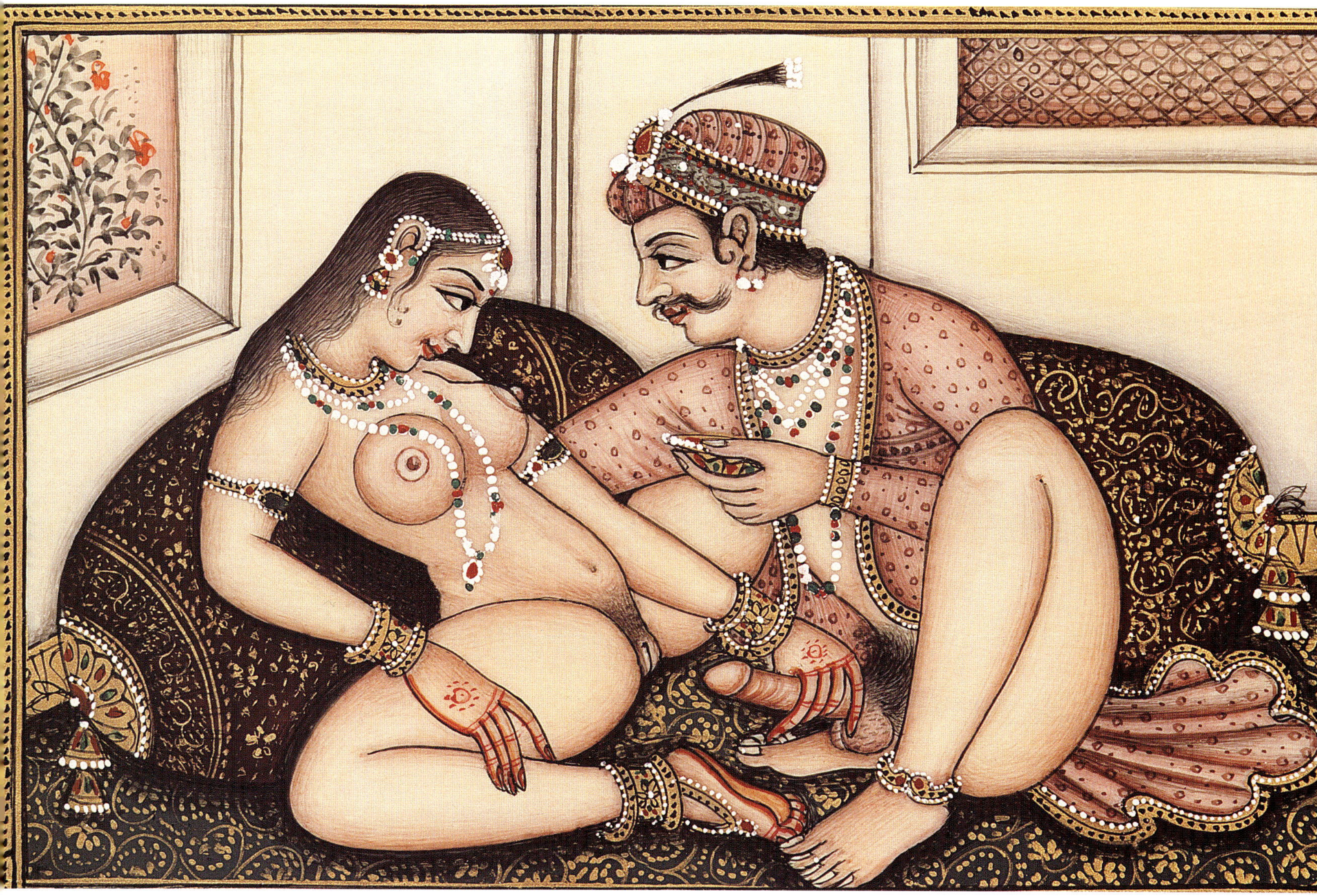

When a lover visits her, a courtesan should entertain him with interesting conversation, be knowledgeable about the arts, give him loving presents, and display her accomplishments and skill in sexual intercourse.

Exchange personal things
And show skill
In sexual enjoyment.

When united
With a lover
Always delight him
By affectionate gifts
Conversation
And the application
Of tender means
Of enjoyment.

On the courtesan living as a wife

A courtesan living as the wife of a man should behave like a chaste woman and do everything to keep him satisfied and happy. She should behave like a wife according to the customs of the community and the nature of the man, give pleasure, behave winningly, and show attachment, but never really get attached.

The extent of a woman's love
Is never known
Even to the objects
Of their affection
On account of its subtlety
And the avarice
And natural intelligence
Of womankind.

Women are rarely known
In their true light
Though they may love men
Become indifferent to them
Give delight
Or abandon them
Even extract from them
All the wealth they possess.

On the means of getting money: on the change in a lover's feelings, and on the way to get rid of him

A wise woman is always aware of her lover's feelings and state of mind from his countenance.

A courtesan should regularly take money from her lover, either by natural and lawful means, or by artifice. Some writers opine that when a courtesan gets as much as she wants from her lover in the normal course, she should not use artifice. Vatsyayana, however, recommended that even when a courtesan gets as much as she wants, artifice will have her gain doubly more and should therefore be used to extort money from a lover. In line with this, the simplest artifice is to speak of some pretended need that will make the lover willingly give what is wanted.

A wise courtesan will constantly remain aware of her lover's state of mind, feelings, and disposition towards her, from changes in his temper, manner, and the colour of his face. The negative signals that she should particularly look out for in her lover, are that:

Courtesans should be beautiful, have good bodies, appreciate good qualities in others, and enjoy wealth and sex with men who desire them.

1. He will give her less than whatever she has asked for, or give her something else altogether, instead.
2. He will keep her in hope with mere promises.
3. He will pretend to do one thing, but actually do another.
4. He will sexually satisfy himself with no concern for her desires.
5. He will forget promises or do other than what he promised.
6. He will have whispered conversations with people, taking care that she does not hear what is being said.
7. He will sleep elsewhere on the pretext of doing something for a friend.
8. He will speak privately with the confidant of a woman he was previously associated with.

Now, when a wise courtesan becomes aware that her lover's attitude towards her is changing, she will take all his best possessions and allow a supposed creditor to take them forcibly away from her, to settle a pretended debt. Then, if the lover is still rich and has always behaved well with her, she should continue treating him with respect, but if he is now poor and destitute, she should get rid of him as if they have never been acquainted with each other.

The various ways in which a courtesan can rid herself of a lover may be any of the following:

1. She may sneeringly describe his habits and vices as disagreeable and reproachable.
2. She may constantly discuss subjects he knows nothing about.
3. She may declare that he is lacking in knowledge and is a fool.
4. She may intentionally hurt his pride.
5. She may seek the company of men superior to him in intelligence.
6. She may demonstrate a disregard for him in all matters.

7. She may speak disparagingly of some faults in other men, which he also has.
8. She may express dissatisfaction with his sexual abilities, techniques, and preferences.
9. She may not give him her mouth to kiss.
10. She may refuse to let him touch her crotch.
11. She may complain about being mishandled.
12. She may hold herself away when embraced.
13. She may lie immobile and indifferent during coitus.
14. She may seek coitus when he is obviously exhausted.
15. She may laugh disparagingly at his love for her.
16. She may not respond to his embraces in any way, or just turn away from them.
17. She may pretend sleepiness when he desires her.
18. She may go out when she sees that he would like to be in her company during the day.
19. She may intentionally misconstrue everything he says.

A woman with a sexual drive as strong as a man's, who is always anxious to acquire experience and knowledge, makes a good courtesan.

*

Men who are celebrated for their sexual prowess are desired by many women.

20. She may laugh when there is no joke, or laugh at something else when he jokes.
21. She may look aside and attend to something else when he speaks to her.
22. She may interrupt his stories to tell her own.
23. She may list his faults and vices, declaring them to be incurable.
24. She may say things to others that are designed to cut him to the quick.
25. She may look away when he comes to her.
26. She may ask him for what he cannot give.
27. She may dismiss him outright.

The courtesan's duty consists
Of forming alliances with men
After due and full consideration
Attaching a man's affections to herself
Obtaining wealth from him
And then dismissing him
When she has taken away
All his possessions.

A courtesan leading
The life of a wife
Is not troubled
With too many lovers
And yet obtains
An abundance of wealth.

On reunion with a former lover

Reunion with a former lover
May be desirable
To separate a particular woman
From a particular man
Or to cause some effect

✻

A courtesan who lives with a man as his wife should be chaste and use her talents to keep him happy and satisfied.

Upon the present lover
Or to win a man
Who gives
Much wealth to a woman
He is excessively attached to
With no regard at all
For her faults.

A courtesan should be agreeable
To the man attached to her
And despise the man
Who cares not for her.
If when living with one man
A messenger comes from another
A courtesan may either refuse to meet him
Or listen to his proposals
Or appoint a time
For the man to visit her
But she should not leave the man
Living with her
Who may be attached to her.

A wise woman should renew connection
With a former lover
Only if satisfied
That good fortune
Love and friendship
Are likely to result
From such a union.
If a man be living
With another woman
Consider well
Before acting.

Some men have or apply medicines to increase their sexual prowess and enhance their pleasure. This allows them to have coitus with many women in one night, and to satisfy their desires.

It should all seem straightforward enough from these verses, but there are several conditions that a wise woman should keep in mind:

1. If a man has left two women, he is fickle and indifferent to the qualities of women.
2. If a man is driven away by one woman, and left by another for a richer man, the first may gain from reunion with him, for if he is attached to her he will give more through vanity, emulation, and a desire to spite the second (however, if the second woman has left him due to his poverty or stinginess, this does not apply).
3. If a man has left a woman and been driven away by the second, the first should first negotiate a good deal for herself before reuniting herself with him.
4. If a man has left a woman and is living with another, the first should consider the matter well before reuniting herself with him.

When old lovers come together after some time, with difficulty, a 'loving coitus' can be carried on for as long as they choose.

5. If a man has been driven away by a woman, and has left another to return to her, she should consider whether he is back because he has no other, whether he only wants to relieve frustrated sexual desires, whether he is trying to win back his confidence and retrieve what he had lost to her, or whether he is just spitefully trying to break her present liaison and then leave her.
6. If a man has been driven away by a woman and is living with another, but still makes overtures to win back the first, reunion of the two may be good for the woman if it had been a mistake to drive him off earlier, if she can use him to

✻

If a man drinks a decoction made of milk, honey and the testicles of a ram or goat, he is supposed to become as virile as a bull and satisfy all women.

get another man, if she likes him as a husband, or she wishes to hurt a rival, or to discredit him for his fickleness.

Various authors recommend that in choosing between a former lover and a new one, the first is preferable since — with disposition and character already known from previous careful observation — he may be easier to please and satisfy. Vatsyayana, however, observed that former lovers, already having given much, will no longer be liberal, and so a new lover is best. On the other hand, he allowed that there will be exceptions to this on account of the differences in the natures of men.

On different kinds of gain

When a courtesan has a surfeit of rich men courting her, she may gain best from setting a nightly tariff on her sexual favours according to the place and the people, her own personal qualities, and the rates charged by others. If, however, great gain can be acquired from a single man, a wise courtesan will unite with him alone, and contrive to live with him as his wife.

Many writers held that in the latter case, when equal gain may be had from either of two men, a courtesan should choose the one who gives her the kind of things she likes. Vatsyayana more practically suggested that in such a case the wise courtesan will choose the one who gives her cash or gold.

When it seems that with equal effort there may be equal gain from either of two potential lovers, a courtesan should ask her friends for advice, and carefully scrutinise the personal qualities of each of the men.

When a courtesan may choose between either a generous lover or one attached to her, some say that she should choose the former. Vatsyayana, however, recommended the latter, with the argument that he can be made generous, just as a miser gives money to a woman he

When lovers come together in the infancy of their love, it is a 'coitus of subsequent love'.

When her husband is away, a woman should be slightly more austere in her lifestyle than when he is there. This is to maintain her reputation and her husband's dignity.

Facing page: *When a woman cannot decide which of her lovers she should choose, she should seek the advice of her friends.*

is fond of. On the other hand, he also advised that if both are attached to her, but one is rich and the other poor, the rich man should be preferred to the poor.

When of two potential lovers, one is generous and the other willing to do service, the generous one should be preferred, for he will not care for what he has given before, while the one willing to do service may think the objective is gained by just doing service once. The wise courtesan will, however, also consider the future good in each option.

When one potential lover is grateful and another liberal, the former is the better choice for a courtesan, for liberal men are generally haughty, plain-spoken, and wanting in consideration. Even after a long relationship, if they see a fault in the woman, or are told lies by her rivals, they will leave abruptly. A grateful man on the other hand, will always have regard for the pains taken to please him. However, a wise courtesan will again consider the future.

When there is a chance of making money, or to satisfy a friend's request, a wise courtesan will consider the future, that money can be obtained tomorrow as well as today, in addition to the fact that the friend may become disaffected if refused. If after this, the courtesan decides to do so, she may refuse the friend by pretending an indisposition or a prior commitment.

Lastly, when there is a chance to make money or avoid disaster, a wise courtesan will avoid disaster, for money is of limited importance, while disaster averted may never threaten again.

Of all the gains that a courtesan may earn, if they be great she should spend some on good public works. If gains are not great, a wise courtesan should spend them on good clothes, food, an attractive house, small indulgences, investments and savings. In any case, a courtesan should sometimes recognise reasons for entertaining a man for just some nominal profit,

When her lover is exhausted, without having achieved orgasm, a woman should lay him on his back and assist him by assuming his role.

taken in a friendly way. But in the parting of ways with a lover, she should endeavour to take as much money from him as she can, as soon as possible. If, however, there is a possibility of profit in a relationship with a lover, a courtesan should think of her future welfare, and live with him as a wife.

In considering present gains
And future welfare
Courtesans should avoid
Men who have gained subsistence
With great difficulty
And those who have become hardhearted
From the power derived
By becoming favourites
Of some other powerful man.
A courtesan should make every effort
To unite
With prosperous and well-to-do people
And those who are dangerous to avoid

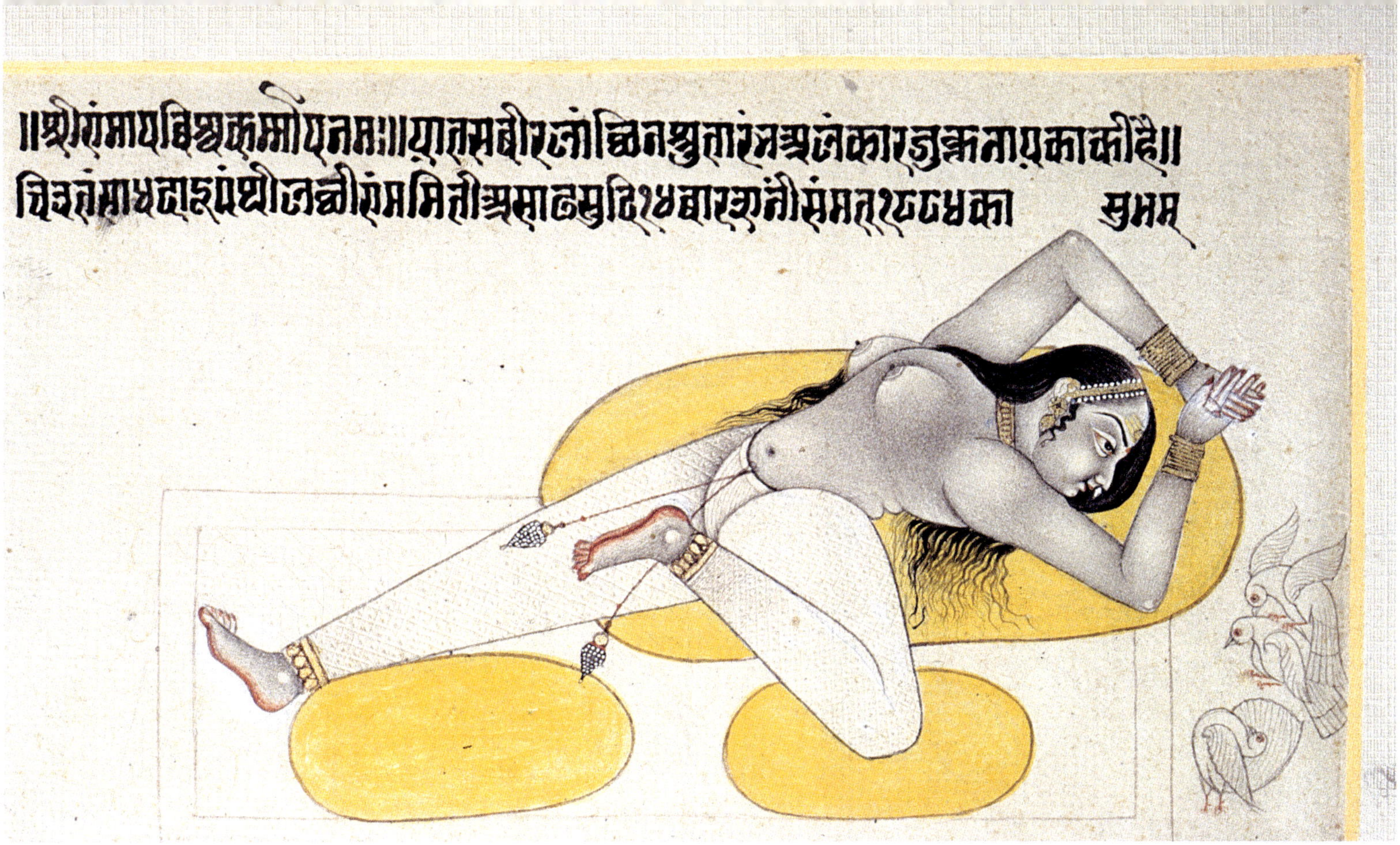

Or slight in any way.
If even at slight cost to themselves
Courtesans should become acquainted
With energetic, liberal-minded men
Who when pleased
Will give large sums of money
For even very little service
Or some little thing.

When a woman quarrels with a man because she is jealous, he should reconcile her with soft words.

Of gains and losses and on different kinds of courtesans

It sometimes happens that while gains are being sought, or are expected to be realised, only losses result from the efforts made. This is caused generally by a weakness of intellect, excessive love, pride, conceit, simplicity, overconfidence, anger, carelessness and recklessness, the influence of an evil genius, or just accidental circumstances.

What may result from this are expenses incurred without result, damage to future good fortune, stoppage of gains about to be realised, loss of what has been already obtained, the acquisition of a sour temper and loss of amiability, and even mental damage, or loss of hair, etc.

In all this, gains are taken to mean those of religious merit, pleasure and wealth. Of the kinds of gain, there may be attendant gains, doubts about whether it is a gain or not, mixed doubts about whether either of the two things will happen, a combination of two results from the same action, and a combination of several gains from the same action. For example:

1. There is an attendant gain when, while acquiring wealth by living with one lover, a courtesan also gets to know other men for future potential gain.
2. There may be simple gain of money unattended by any other gains.
3. When accepting money from a man other than her lover, a courtesan may gain little, with the possible attendant loss of future good from her lover, the affection of a man attached to her, and the love of people who respect her. She may also destroy the possibility of her future association with good people, and destroy her own future good fortune.
4. There may be loss of wealth attended by potential future good fortune when a courtesan unites with a great man or an avaricious man of power, at her own expense, to divert misfortune or remove a threat to her accumulated fortune.
5. There is loss unattended by any gain when a courtesan unites at her expense with a man who is stingy, proud of his looks, and ungrateful, yet skilled in winning over the hearts of others.
6. When a courtesan at her own expense unites with such a man, who is also powerful by association with others, and extracts no commitment at all from him, she will have a loss attended by other losses.

It has been said that the extent of a woman's love is never known, even by those she loves.

Doubts about gains may be of the following kinds:

1. A courtesan may have doubts about gaining wealth when she is uncertain about how much a man will give or spend on her.
2. She may have doubts on the issue of morality when abandoning a man because he has nothing left after she has taken everything she could from him.

A woman who has gained the affection of her husband must respect and revere him and also his gods.

3. She may have doubts about the pleasure to be derived from seducing a married man or a low one, when her lovers are not to her liking.
4. She may have doubts about loss of wealth when she fears that a powerful and low-principled man may take advantage of her being civil to him.
5. She may have doubts about the moral implications of leaving a man who loves her, because he will suffer.
6. She may have doubts about the loss of pleasure when uncertain about whether she will create disaffection in a man by speaking out and revealing her love for him.

Below and facing page: *When consorting with men, a courtesan should persuade him to give her money as well as pleasure.*

Mixed doubts may be as follows:

1. A courtesan may have mixed doubts about potential gains or losses when uniting with a powerful man, or a stranger of unknown disposition introduced to her by her lover.
2. She may have mixed doubts on moral grounds when uniting with a religious student or cleric because the man is madly in love with her, and can only thus be saved.
3. She may have mixed doubts about gains or losses when uniting with a man on the basis of hearsay rather than a personal assessment.

Uddalika added to all this that there may be gains and losses on both sides from an association, and cited the following examples:

1. There may be gain of both wealth and pleasure in life with a lover.
2. There will be losses on both sides with a lover who is maintained at a courtesan's own expense, and who also takes back what he had previously given her.
3. There may be doubts on both sides about whether a new acquaintance will or will not grow attached to the courtesan, and whether he will give her anything at all if he is won over.

4. There may be doubts about reunion with an old lover or enemy, who has been won over at her own expense, for the courtesan may be uncertain about whether he will carry with him an old grudge, or angrily take back what he had given her before.

Babhravya's examples about gains and losses on both sides are as follows:

1. There is gain on both sides when a courtesan gets money from a man she may or may not meet.
2. There is a loss on both sides when a courtesan goes to a man at her own expense because there is a potential greater loss in not doing so.
3. There is a doubt on both sides when a courtesan is uncertain about the potential gains in uniting with either one man or the other.
4. There is a doubt on both sides when a courtesan goes at her own expense to an old

Group sex, though not common, was not unknown. It was mainly rich and powerful men who indulged in it.

enemy, for she may be uncertain whether he will take back what she has earlier gained from him, or will cause her some other disaster.

Of all gains and losses, there are but four combinations: there may be gain on one side and loss on the other; there may be loss on one side and gain on the other; there may be gain on both sides, and there may be loss on both sides.

After having considered everything well, and after having taken counsel from her friends, a wise courtesan will always opt to acquire gain, the chance of great gain, and the opportunity of warding off potential disaster. Religious merit and pleasure should also be formed into separate combinations, like those of wealth, and then all should be combined together to form new combinations for consideration.

When consorting with men, a courtesan should cause each to provide her with money as well as pleasure. When young men make advances with obvious delight in having met the woman, she should wisely think of what may be accomplished through them. In all her affairs, a wise woman will only act after considering all her own doubts about gains and losses, with reference to wealth, religious merits and pleasures.

Of the various kinds of courtesans, it can be said that there are bawds, female attendants, unchaste women, dancing girls, female artisans, women who have left their families, women living off their beauty, and finally, the straightforward courtesan who does not pretend to be anything else. Different kinds of courtesans are acquainted with different kinds of men, but all should consider ways of getting money from them, pleasing them, winning them,

It has been said that a man who is well versed in the sixty-four divisions of the Kamasutra becomes a leader in any society, is respected by the learned, the cunning and by courtesans.

separating from them, and reuniting with them. They should also always consider particular gains and losses, attendant gains and losses, and doubts, in accordance with several conditions.

Lovers should be constantly aware of each other's responses during lovemaking — what is liked and what is not.

Facing page: *While making love, a man should caress and press those parts of a woman's body that she looks at.*

Men want pleasure
While women want security
So this part
Treating of the ways
To gain wealth
Should be studied.
There are some women
Who seek love

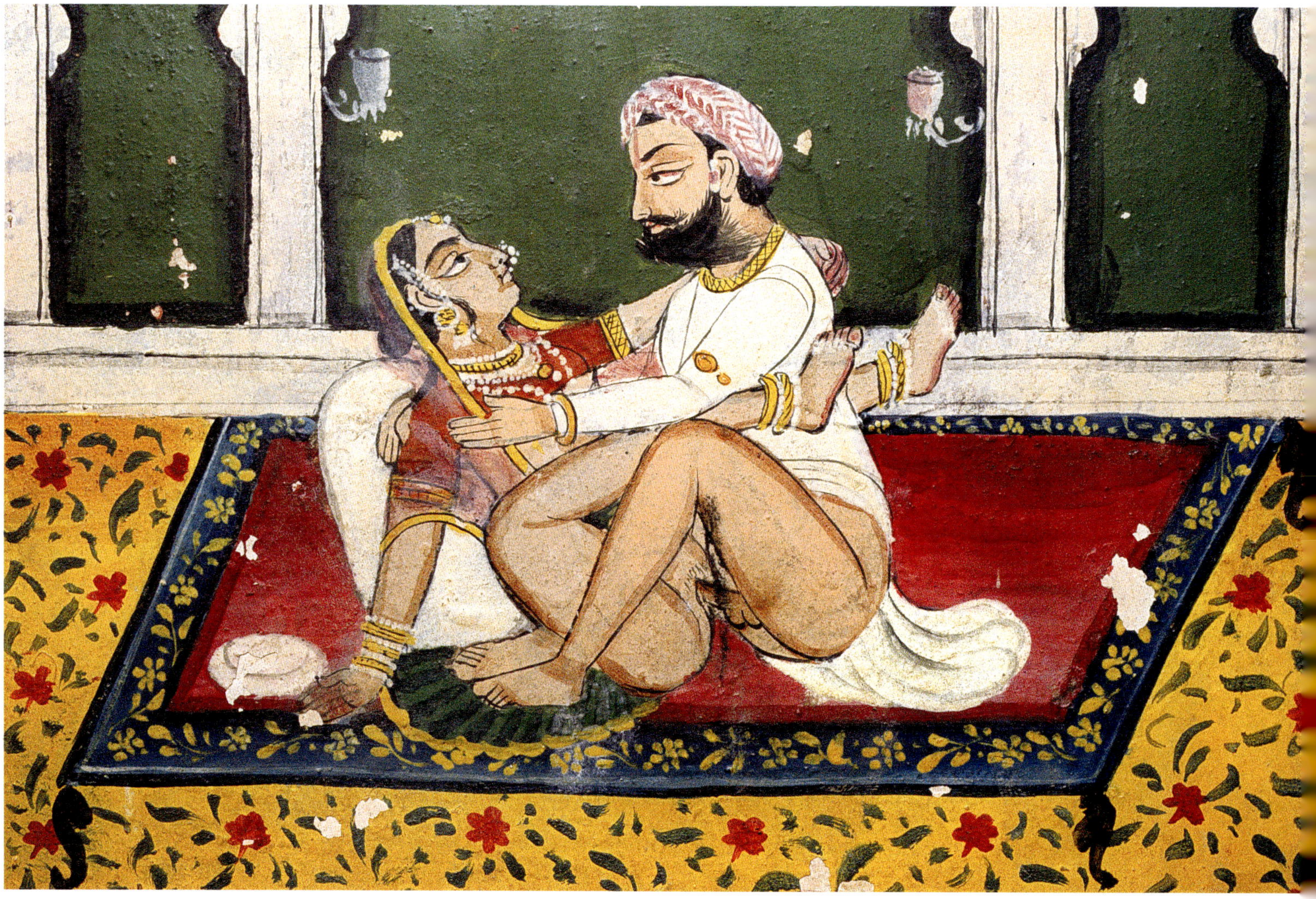

And some who seek money.
For the former
The ways of love
Have been told in previous chapters
While the ways of getting money
As practised by courtesans
Are described
In this part.

The means of producing love
And sexual vigour
Should be learned
From the science of medicine
From literature
From masters of magic
And from close relatives.
No means should be used
Which are doubtful in their effect
Likely to cause bodily injury
Involving the death of animals
Or which bring us into contact
With impure things.

Only such means should be used
As are acknowledged to be good
And approved of by respectable people
And friends.

There have been uncounted mechanical aids used in coitus through the centuries, and today there is an entire industry devoted to their production. One must, however, be very clear that these industries cater to a negligible microcosm of all the world's lovers. If lovers — after considering the matter fully and finding the notion agreeable to both — decide to use such devices, they should take care that it is completely safe to do so.

Facing page and above:
Either or both the lovers can indulge in a 'coitus of transferred love' by imagining his or her partner to be someone else.

Lovers who think that the man's phallus is too small for the woman will often find that extended foreplay directly on the woman's vagina will lead to better mutual satisfaction in coitus. However, if both are agreed that they would like to try a mechanical embellishment, for whatever reason, they may proceed in a variety of ways.

Some recommendations from over two thousand years ago may still be appropriate today, but one cannot overstate the need of consideration for safety and a complete accord of intent in both lovers. Beware that an absence of the latter will almost certainly have the dissenter view the initiator as a pervert, if he or she were to pursue the case beyond a reasonable degree.

It is said that in ancient Rome women sometimes even inserted the tails of live fish or the heads of live snakes into their vaginas for sexual stimulation, but it will be clear to the reader that in all this, the notion of a loving coitus between lovers is easily lost sight of. Lovers would therefore do well to always take care that the man has some chance of at least some little stimulation of his phallus by contact with the woman's vagina, or a brand-new problem may arise in the relationship.

In some communities in the world, operations have been routinely performed to embed objects things in the skin of men's phalluses, to produce a bumpy surface. Perforations have been made in the foreskin, and even in the phallus, to allow the man to wear some device (one of them is not surprisingly called the 'goad of an elephant') which will rub more strongly against the insides of a woman's vagina during coitus. A somewhat simpler operation has been performed in some societies to partially circumcise a man so as to leave his foreskin as a flap on his phallus.

An intelligent man who depends on his own ability, and carefully observes the thoughts of women, is usually successful with them. ***Facing page:*** *When a woman lies on your bed, abstracted by your touch and conversation, loosen the fastening of her dress and undergarments.*

There is really no way that these practices can be recommended outside the societies in which they exist.

What may be enjoyable for some healthy lovers, however, are the various massage oils that cause a tingling sensation, or one of heat or cold, when applied to the skin. Beyond this, lovers will find that all the sexual aids and devices needed for good coitus are already to be found in just the two of them.

The passionate acts, amorous gesticulations, and the movements of lovemaking cannot be defined — they are as irregular as dreams.
Facing page: *Although a woman may be reserved and conceal her feelings, when she is atop a man she shows all her love and desire.*
Pages 142-143: *The most remarkable aspect of the Kamasutra is its attitude of equality between men and women in matters of sexual love. This attitude is embodied in the term* sam bhoga, *which means 'enjoying together, enjoying in harmony'.*

।गीतगोविंदरोपत्र॥२२६॥ अह्लो निर्दिप॥सखी राधिकाप्रतें कहे है॥यो
मीमांते॥ नेत्ररे विषे अंजन करे है॥ कर्णरे विषे तमालरा प्रसव गुंछे है॥ धरे
करे है॥ स्त्रियांकीसी है॥ अति धूर्त्त है॥ वलै गतिरे विषे मंदगत है॥ अंधकार

कार सुंदर हैं नेत्र जीणं राइ सी स्त्रीयां हैं अंग प्रत्यंग प्रते आलिंगन करे है ॥
मस्तक रे विषे स्यांम कमल री माला हैं करे है ॥ कुच रे विषे कस्तूरी थी पत्रिक
सो है ॥ स्यांम वस्त्र सरीषो है ॥

All rights are reserved. No part of this publication may be
transmitted or reproduced in any form or by any means
without the prior permission of the publisher.

ISBN: 0-86288-557-4

This edition published in 2003
Greenwich Editions
10 Blenheim Court, Brevery Road
London, N7 9N T

A member of the Chrysalis Group plc

© Roli & Janssen BV 2001

Published in India by Roli Books
in arrangement with Roli & Janssen BV
M-75, Greater Kailash II (Market)
New Delhi 110 048, India.
Phones: (011) 6442271, 6462782, 6460886
Fax: (011) 6467185, E-mail: roli@vsnl.com
Website: rolibooks.com

TEXT: Shankar Barua

PHOTO CREDITS:
Aditya Patankar: pages 33, 38, 42, 64, 107, 127
Dheeraj Paul: pages 2, 3, 70-71
Lance Dane: pages 52, 53
M.D. Sharma: pages 55, 80, 81, 86, 98, 128, 129, 130, 139
Roli Books Collection: pages 4, 12, 13, 16, 17, 19, 22, 27, 30, 32, 34, 35, 36, 37, 39, 40-41, 43, 44, 45, 46, 47, 49, 50, 51, 54, 56, 57, 58, 59, 60, 61, 62, 63, 65, 66, 67, 68, 69, 77, 82-83, 84, 94-95, 96, 97, 99, 100-101, 102-103, 104, 105, 106, 108, 109, 112, 114, 115, 116, 117, 118, 119, 120, 121, 122, 123, 124, 125, 126, 131, 132, 133, 134, 136, 140, 142-143
Victoria & Albert Museum, London: pages 1, 5, 6-7, 8-9, 10, 14-15, 18, 20-21, 23, 24-25, 26, 28-29, 72, 74-75, 76, 78, 79, 87, 88, 90, 91, 92-93, 110, 113, 135

DESIGN: Inkspot

Printed and bound in Singapore